# TRANSFOR
# MOMENTS

*Edited by*
*Scarlett MccGwire*

**VIRAGO UPSTARTS**

Published by VIRAGO PRESS Limited 1989
20–23 Mandela Street, Camden Town, LONDON NW1 0HQ

This collection and introduction copyright © Scarlett MccGwire 1989
Copyright © in each contribution held by the author 1989

*A CIP Catalogue record for this book
is available from the British Library*

Printed in Great Britain by
The Guernsey Press Ltd, C.I.

For Cherry Bevan, Kate Allott,
Cesilie Tandero and Meg Westley –
my teenage friends.

# CONTENTS

Acknowledgements    *viii*

Introduction    *ix*

Frock Monster in Disco Error    *Cath Carroll*    *1*

Rebel with a Cause    *Sarjeet Kaur-Chaunder*    *9*

Out of the Cocoon    *Melanie McFadyean*    *16*

She's Leaving Home    *Shreela Ghosh*    *31*

And Still I Rise    *Maya Angelou*    *39*

I Will Go to London, I Will    *Scarlett MccGwire*    *54*

Love in the Warsaw Ghetto    *Janina Bauman*    *64*

Derry's Blue Suede Shoes    *Nell McCafferty*    *77*

From Suicide to Survival    *Eileen Fairweather*    *84*

Grandmother's Secret    *Sally Morgan*    *95*

Sex and Sexuality    *Clare Bayley*    *110*

An Argentinian Diary    *Alicia Partnoy*    *120*

Out of the Well of Loneliness    *Julia Robertson*    *127*

The Jimi Hendrix Experience    *Charlotte Greig*    *133*

Loving You    *Priscilla Presley*    *140*

The Italian Lesson    *Anne Karpf*    *148*

Young, Gifted and Black    *Diane Abbott*    *153*

DO NOT STAND AT MY GRAVE AND CRY
I AM NOT HERE, I DID NOT DIE!

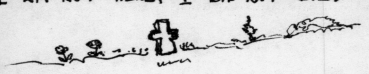

*Acknowledgements*

I would like to thank Century Hutchinson and Ed Victor for permission to use an extract from Priscilla Beaulieu Presley's *Elvis and Me*; Freemantle Press for the extract from Sally Morgan's *My Place*; and Random House for the extract from Maya Angelou's *I Know Why the Caged Bird Sings*.

# INTRODUCTION

When Virago asked me to edit this book I jumped at the idea. I thought that a collection of women looking back on their teenage years and picking out the incidents which helped shape them as the people they are today would make fascinating reading. It was the sort of book I would have been grateful for during my school years to prove there is real life after adolescence.

I wanted all sorts of different stories, so I wrote to women with a multitude of backgrounds – class, colour, religion, age and region where they grew up – to cover a range of experiences. I asked them to write about a 'transforming moment': an event which in some way changed the course of their lives and influenced what they have become as adults. The stories which came back reflect the many upbringings. Many contain feelings we all have, though others – like Janina Bauman's experience as a Jew in the Warsaw ghetto during the war or Alicia Partnoy being arrested by the Argentinian junta – are, luckily, far removed from many of us.

I remember all too clearly sitting in my boarding school in rural Dorset wondering when I could join the world outside, always feeling I was missing out. Cath Carroll's piece speaks vividly of all the teenage frustration and that particular shame of being 'someone who lived with her parents'. Melanie McFadyean's patchwork of moments shows the gradual growth from girl to woman.

The stories have a sadness to them, which ironically I find rather cheering, discovering that I was not alone in my unhappiness. Perhaps that unspecific discontent almost comes with the age? However, the transforming moments are always positive, beginning to pull away from that restless depression to exert some control over the authors' lives.

The pieces reflect a whole range of problems with their partial solutions. Many of us have to leave home before we begin to make sense of our lives – though few as dramatically as Shreela Ghosh, who just left a note for her father, or with as much to leave as Eileen Fairweather in a home of mental and physical abuse, who with her suicide attempt tried to opt for a more final solution. Anne Karpf left the country briefly and discovered that in Italy she could successfully try being the person she had always wished to be.

Sally Morgan and Julia Robertson started their teenage years refusing to acknowledge any differences between them and their school friends: it was only realising their particular individuality – in Sally's case her aborigine background; for Julia her lesbianism – which freed them to deal with life honestly. Whereas Clare Bayley surprised herself with both the power and pleasure of her sexuality, which led her to a long hard look at men and women's relationships.

For Sarjeet Kaur-Chaunder and Maya Angelou it was the discovery of racism within the very fabric of society and the determination to beat it which helped them to claim back their lives on their own terms.

And what is being a teenager without music? Charlotte Greig saw the raw side of life through Jimi Hendrix. For Nell McCafferty Elvis Presley brought life to Derry on dreary Sundays, while Priscilla Beaulieu fell in love with, and eventually married him.

They are all wonderful stories in their own right; however, I hope they also provide an inspiration for those trying to find themselves, for those who are trying to define themselves instead of being told what sort of a person they are by parents and teachers. For Diane Abbott it was a matter of deciding what she wanted to do and doing it.

I would like to thank all the authors who have contributed to this book: for dredging out memories that some would rather have left alone; for the patience of those who delivered immediately and then had the long wait for publication; and those who worked and reworked their pieces.

My particular thanks to Lennie Goodings from Virago for bearing with me during the many periods when it looked as though the book was never going to happen, and her enthusiasm whenever I managed another spurt of activity. It was Christian's gentle lecture which made me finally pull myself together and get down to it: Thank you. And a special mention for Pascoe.

# CATH CARROLL

## *Frock Monster in Disco Error*

**C**ath Carroll was born in summer 1960 at Chipping Sodbury Cottage Hospital during one of her father's regional postings. He is an accountant turned market trader; her mother is an audiotypist. The riotous showbiz background is as follows: parents owned two Gene Autrey records, two Herb Alpert and stacks of The Dubliners. Also, mother sang in a duo in Irish clubs prior to marriage and a distant grandparent once played the organ in a Midlands cathedral.

She began her schooling in Wales, learnt the Welsh for 'hole', 'yes' and 'yuk', and commenced serious school in the family homelands of Lancashire. Left law degree, horrified by Lord Denning, to become a postwoman and wrote with partner Liz Naylor for Manchester fanzine City Fun. Left post office, horrified by modifications in uniform, to concentrate on playing with self-taught noise band Gay Animals.

Accident of fate made her north-west correspondent for the New Musical Express. She then moved with cat, group and crowbar to London, wrote occasionally for Him, Marxism Today, and The Wire, as well as the gossip column at the NME. Her group Miaow made several independent singles (tepidly received) and she is now signed to Factory Records as a solo artist. Her obsessions are Victorian railway stations and Latin America; her ambitions, too embarrassing to print.

It may sound stupid – especially since I was some time past the age of fourteen – but I really thought it would never happen to me. I'd watch the older girls at my school and most of the girls in my class and wonder why they seemed so carefree, so unperturbed by the monstrous handicap that nature was bestowing upon them. Puberty was another country as far as I was concerned and I was convinced it would stay that way. I guess I just assumed that they'd wanted it to happen to them and so down came the magic Hormone Fairy and everyone went home happy. Being a sporty brat, I could not afford to be encumbered with breasts that went *boing* and flesh with a mind of its own. That was no way to impress the talent scout for Manchester United Football Club (just in case he happened to be passing our hockey field . . .). Recognising me as a sporty brat who needed to be taught a lesson, the magic Hormone Fairy paid me a stern visit.

What can you do? Go 'Excuse me, I don't go to discos, I don't go out with boys. I am going to be the first fourteen-year-old on the Man. Utd first team (oh, heady daydreams) – but not with *these things*. Give them to my friend Nancy, who's complaining that she can't fill her bra.' Nope, you can't. So I was lumbered with a body and biology that just didn't belong to me. It's not that I thought that women's bodies were ugly, they looked fine on other girls, but they were useless for the acts of athletic perversion that I had in mind. And thus one (inevitable) transforming moment sent me sick as a parrot, [Brian,] into the beginning of a *real* change. At the end of this adolescence I'd got to feeling so out of place with everything that I was driven out of a meagre introversion into an action that changed my life – or rather gave me the chance to realise the main theme from my lurid catalogue of fantasies. I should have done it sooner, but I just didn't know how.

I didn't know *anything*. Well, except for what my mother taught me about good manners, the Catholic Church and the iniquities suffered by the trade-union movement. Plus a whole lot of Latin verbs which were obviously going to give my social life no end of a boost. The reason it took so long to get to where I wanted to be was merely a reference problem born from a stunted sense of adventure and an isolated existence. Talking to people now – all sorts of people – most of them seem to have worked out some sort of customised social structure, or at least knew where it existed, long before the age of seventeen. I discovered it quite by accident whilst trying to find Fab-208-Radio-Luxembourg on my parents' geriatric radio. The only station it was picking up that night was Radio Two which, after ten o'clock, twinned with Radio One for John Peel's show. This was some time in 1978. The last time I'd tried out John Peel had been four years ago when he was playing some gruesome progressive rock track that took up the whole programme (well . . .) and caused me to file him alongside Alan Freeman as someone who actively encouraged those drearily depressing guitarists with long hair. There was only one sound more depressing than those *addle-addle-nee-oww* records, and that was the combined drone of a racing commentary and the washing machine on a wet afternoon. If only I'd listened to John Peel again sooner. All the friends I have now did. I was about as resourceful and adventurous as a piece of plankton. And that sentence degrades plankton.

I'd tuned in that night in the middle of a record which was belting along like nobody's business, with guitars playing not only speedy square shapes but something that I might be able to reconstruct on the previously uncooperative acoustic guitar that had arrived as requested two Christmases before. And then came the guitar break. It was played on one string and on practically one note. Revelation! It wasn't like a religious experience or anything, significant moments never are. It's that slow dawning of recognition, recognition of something familiar from which one has become inexplicably estranged – except, of course, that it isn't at all familiar. Anyway, the record ('What Do I Get' by Buzzcocks) ended with me being bodily wrapped around the radio in case any information tried to escape. I'd received my first instructions.

For the first time I'd found something in contemporary culture that I could understand. I didn't know a thing about the group except that they lived in Manchester. THEY LIVED IN MANCHESTER! They actually still lived around the city where I went to school. After years thinking that the only records worth listening to were made by people who either lived in America or were dead I find that the best group in the world (a) were not yet inaccessible pop stars and (b) lived somewhere in the same telephone directory area as my parents. I forget what I did the next day; it was a school day and doubtless the carrier of some fresh hell. I went home on the bus as usual, though I checked the streets for those like-minded people who I now knew existed. I didn't see them, but the streets looked a lot more interesting all of a sudden. That was Manchester. I had a problem: I lived in Stockport. Not even in the town. In a residential suburb with no night bus and no one I knew. But the idea of getting out and outside my bedroom/schoolroom existence suddenly seemed practicable just because I'd found something to aim for.

Ah, Stockport, so much to answer for. A run-down industrial centre six miles out of Manchester that revived its economy with one of those late-sixties shopping precinct plagues built to service the council estates (walking distance) and the residential satellite settlements (twenty minutes in a Ford Cortina). You meet a lot of people who *come* from Stockport, but it's not one of those places young people move into unless they want to give their lawn sprinkler a good start in life. Not like Salford or Moss Side or Newton Heath, lesser centres of commerce, but with rooms to let and close enough to the city centre to benefit from a cultural overspill. Stockport, blooming lividly, is for families. It had a couple of non-chainstore record shops, but in the mid seventies these were patronised by those initiated into the relevant seventies sub-cults, i.e. they didn't get bought clothes from British Home Stores by their parents and they had hair*styles*. In short, Stockport was like most other towns: a bad backdrop to a blighted adolescence. An ignorable backdrop if you happened to be one of those weirdie children of Satan who had a grand time in your teenage years.

Having been excellently indulgent in allowing us to spend most of our childhood either up a tree or grunting with fellow troglodytes in a building-site trench, our parents changed tack and dragged their three offspring out of that rural cradle and into the family homelands of the north-west of England. We stopped off in Rochdale for six months, renting a bungalow furnished with miniature liqueurs and ships in bottles in an estate full of the same. Next door were boy children of corresponding ages, and after school we all got along famously, getting stuck up trees and drinking the liqueurs from the bottles. At school we would spend our lunch hours in our respective play areas vomiting in fear of the threats of decapitation and disembowelling that were levelled against us because of our mutant Ipswich-Oldham accents. The abrasive behaviour of the bellowing male teachers, with their hands and canes in perpetual motion, also had us retching in terror, but it gave you a sense of belonging. When the murder threats were suspended you could argue about football and lots of other crap. Then our parents moved us all to Quiet Hell, a block full of grown-ups and dogs. I was bused out to a grammar school in the city – miles out. The two friends I met there – well, we didn't so much meet as get thrown together, as we were the ones left hanging around the touchlines whenever the class had to organise itself for team activities – lived on the other side of the city, so I hardly ever saw them out of school and anyway they had friends in their neighbourhood. Oh dear, whine, whine.

There I was, a social retard, incapable of sustaining – let alone initiating – a conversation with my peers unless it involved Olga Korbut or ornithology. The local youth club was out of the question, since most of the people who went there were the ones from the local school who used to meet me off the school bus and bully my uniform (hat and scarf but rarely me; Dada was enjoying a renaissance in east Stockport). So that left the Girl Guides. NO THANKS! I wanted to join the Scouts.

I felt OK in boys' company, but girls – *girl* girls, *proper* girls

5

– always made me feel grubby and gauche. The female personality, no matter what its shading, sent me into an instant state of submission, and I still don't know why. I attended an all-girls school, so I spent a lot of time cringing and submitting and feeling grubby. The only escape was in sports. My friend Gilly and I stayed behind after school for all manner of physical culture. Gilly had a thing about the gym mistress and I hung round her too, hoping she'd teach me the back flip. This unnatural behaviour was noted by our fellows, and the tag *lezzie* attached itself to us. Gilly wasn't too bothered; she was better than I was at living in a world of her own. I minded just because it was another reason to be ostracised. We did, I suppose, have some kind of embryonic relationship, but we had a long, long way to go before qualifying as lesbians.

Then womanhood burgeoned and I abandoned sport. Eventually I tried to join in the hormone ritual, wearing make-up, heels and dreadful, dreadful dresses and trying to get interested in the opposite sex. The latter was almost as great a disaster as the dressing up. Cultural alienation meant that I wasn't impressed by the boys of the 1970s. I wanted ones like they had in the 1940s and 1950s. And the boys from the 1970s certainly weren't impressed by me because I was a frump and a fright and felt like a drag queen. Anyway, Dad wouldn't let me go out with boys, so that was that. It let me off the hook.

The only way to blot out the horror and social ineptitude of school hours was to closet myself in my bedroom and listen to Elvis Presley songs I'd taped off the radio. I wanted to be an Elvis impersonator. Or a rockabilly guitarist. Then, for some unfathomable reason, I acquired three Elton John records. I didn't want to be in *his* band. My hormones, having nothing better to do with their time, were plotting romance. All wishes for a secret love tryst with Elton John went right out of the window when I discovered another band I wanted to be in: the Four Seasons. It was getting better. At least that group were still around . . . I asked a few acquaintances in my class if they wanted to form a group. A couple wanted to form a Christian folk duo. I went back to my bedroom and the Elvis impersonations. By the time I accidentally discovered John Peel and Buzzcocks, I was auditioning myself for Manhattan Transfer. And that was when everything started to change.

For the first year I just walked round Manchester and hovered outside record shops. Although I'd at last acquired a pair of drainpipe jeans and some sneakers, I still wasn't up to the cadaverous punk chic that most other people seemed to manage. I'd buy an occasional record and feel sheepish because everyone in the shop must have known that THIS PERSON LIVES WITH HER PARENTS. That was not very punk. At all. I hoped and hoped that one day someone would come up to me and demand that I join their group. In the meantime I spent all other out-of-school hours jumping up and down in the garage to the John Peel Show. Or daydreaming about being places other than Stockport. Consequently my academic career slumped and my poor parents were left surveying the wreckage. I went to Manchester Polytechnic to do law, convinced that I'd find someone there who'd be in a band. Nope. Most were Tories who just wanted to get their qualification and then piss off to make pots of money. The others could see that THIS PERSON LIVES AT HOME WITH HER PARENTS. Eventually the punk rock catechism clicked: Do It Yourself. I persuaded my bemused father to put up a loan for an electric guitar. The next day I went back to buy an amplifier and lead because I thought you just plugged the guitar in at the mains like they did in *The Beano*. What a divvy, eh? Then came the final act of desperation. I put an ad in *Sounds* for people to join my group. The sub-text to that was that I wanted friends.

That's how I met Liz, who was a few squares ahead on the social board game but, like me, needed an ally. She'd suffered worse horrors at school through daring to dress as she pleased. This landed her in a psychiatric unit for young homosexuals. She was the first person I'd met who hadn't clung to the rails of academic progress. I was still going through the motions like a headless chicken. At first her impulsiveness scared me, but she knew what she was doing. She made me realise there was another way that was worth taking risks for. I abandoned the idea of a career in community law; I'd only have ended up being a secret Elvis impersonator again. She introduced me to Oxfam shops. I took my father's old suit and chopped my hair off. We wore ties and cuff links and starched our collars. People thought we were weird punks. We thought we were Radclyffe Hall. The first time I wore men's clothes was a moment of ecstatic liberation. It had nothing to do with wanting to be men, and in the end, nothing to do with our sexuality. It just felt right.

And so . . . we moved into a council flat, wrote together, plotted together, hated each other but planned to take over the world. We entered a second adolescence that made sense of the horrors of the first. We went out on a limb. That was not very pleasant sometimes. Sometimes I wanted to kill her. The feeling was mutual. But we'd both found a lifestyle that gave us freedom and self-determination. We'd both escaped from our bedroom lives in east Stockport. A miracle. We wrote for a fanzine, then that led us to the *NME*. We moved the group to London and split up. Eventually we were reconciled. It's taken ten years to get anywhere near a record contract, but at least in that time I've learnt how to cope with being female on my own terms. If it hadn't been for meeting Liz and hearing the Buzzcocks, I guess I'd have found a way out of the isolation somehow. But the police would have had to be called.

# SARJEET KAUR-CHAUNDER

## *Rebel with a Cause*

I am twenty-three years old, five foot tall, slim with fair skin, black hair and black eyes. I wear Indian traditional fashion clothes and sometimes suits; I used to wear skirts before my marriage, but now I feel different, I just couldn't go out in skirts. I always make my own suits.

I was born in New Cross Hospital Wolverhampton, which is where I had my children, Zackie and Angie. I have two younger sisters: one is married with children and the other is still at Cotton Hills School, where I used to go. I have two older brothers who are married with families. My parents don't live far from my house.

I have done various jobs since I left school at sixteen, and now make clothes in a factory.

It was not love at first sight between Som and me – not quite. I was shopping in Marks and Spencer's with a friend when I first met him. She pointed him out to me, and although I had not met him I knew who he was. She wanted to go and speak to him but I tried to stop her approaching him, as I felt so shy. I was not used to talking to boys whom I did not know well, but she was already going out with boys and found them easy to approach: she did not understand my reticence. She would not listen to my pleading not to go up to him and just pulled me with her as she walked towards him.

She said 'Hello', then after a few minutes of chat suggested that we all went for a cup of coffee. We went to a nearby Wimpy Bar and as Som started talking to me my shyness started dissolving and I found myself happily chattering away to him – so much so, I almost forgot about my friend being there.

I was working as a clerk in the council's housing department, at the Civic Centre, and he arranged to meet me the next day for lunch. It just seemed natural that he picked me up after work and walked me home in the evening – and when I started going out with him in the evenings it just seemed natural that I should spend all my free time with him. My parents did not know; they would have killed me if they had found out – in the evenings I just told them I was going over to see a girlfriend.

I decided to marry him about two weeks after we met. I just knew he was right for me.

I had been thinking about marriage because I knew my parents were looking for a boy for me. They had given me the choice between one from India or England. I had opted for a British boy because boys from India are really old-fashioned and I knew they would not like me to wear what I wanted. I also wanted my husband to be just like a British person, like me, not to come from a foreign country. I wanted a husband who dressed up nicely and cut his hair, and the Indian men I knew did not do that.

It never struck me till years after we had married that choosing Som went against all this, for he had been over here only a matter of weeks.

As I had already left school my parents wanted me married. In the Indian culture parents like to marry girls off quickly, before they are twenty or as soon as they leave school. So I knew they would find me a husband soon.

We were sitting in a pub when I realised I did not want my parents to choose my husband, I had already decided. I could not imagine having to live with another man after I discovered Som. He already seemed a permanent part of my life.

I said to Som: 'I think we should get married.'

He said: 'Well, if you think we should, then we will.'

I said: 'Yes, I'm sure.'

We got very excited and drank some more, then when they

called last orders I realised what the time was and I was frightened to go home because it was so late.

I told Som I was scared my parents were going to beat me.

'They can't beat you, they can't.'

'I know they will, I know my parents.'

When I got home I had to face them. Dad was in a temper and Mum was worried sick waiting up for me.

My Dad said: 'Where have you been?'

'Out.'

'Where?'

'In the pub.'

'What were you doing in the pub? Girls don't go into pubs.'

'Well, I did.'

'Who did you go with?'

I could not lie and say I was with a girl, so I just said: 'A boy.'

'What boy?'

'My boyfriend.'

'Boyfriend?'

'Yes. And I want to get married to him.'

'What do you mean you want to get married to him? You can't choose your own husband. You will get married to the boy I find for you.'

I was furious and told him I would do what I wanted with my life, not what he dictated. And I marched upstairs. I heard my mum telling my dad to cool down and we would all talk about it in the morning.

When I came downstairs the next morning, Mum said: 'Were you drunk last night?'

'A bit.'

'Do you remember what you said?'

'I know what happened.'

'Is it true?'

'Yeah. I want to get married to him.'

'In the Indian culture girls can have boyfriends, but they

can't get married to them. Everybody will talk about our family if you get married to him. I want you to get married to a boy we choose.'

'No. I want to get married to him. I want you to arrange it, just as if it was a normal marriage. Then nobody will find out it is a love marriage.'

My mum agreed to talk to my dad and they arranged it all for us. We were married at an Indian temple.

My parents had come over from India and their marriage had been traditionally arranged by their parents. I think they have been happy with it, and it certainly never occurred to them that there was another way. My father works at the Goodyear factory making tyres and my mother stays at home.

When they had children we were brought up as part of a traditional Indian family – yet not quite. For we were not in India and we were surrounded by British culture. We were a close family and we were expected not to do anything to bring the family into disrepute, but we were not expected to mix only within the Indian community. My parents were not really strict: they let me wear what I liked and my sisters and I used to go out a lot.

I went to Carleton Hill Comprehensive in Wolverhampton, which I really enjoyed. I had friends there, white and Black, but never had a boyfriend. I was shy with boys; in fact I was shy with everyone except my friends. I remember skiving off drama because I was so scared of doing anything in front of the class. I knew that people saw me as a timid little Indian girl, yet on the inside I just wanted to be free, to go where I wanted and do what I wanted. I wanted to experience everything life had to offer. That was why I left school as soon as I could: the Easter after my sixteenth birthday, with no qualifications at all. I just wanted to get out and enjoy life. I thought being out of school would give me freedom, but now I look back and wish I had stayed to take those exams.

\* \* \*

When I married Som I knew very little about him or his background – I was so much in love, none of it seemed to matter. He had come over to England from India quite recently for a holiday and was staying with his sister, who lived about five minutes' walk away from my parents' home. Back in India he had four older sisters and two younger ones. He had been a photographer and now hoped to start a business here.

There had never been any question about where we would settle. Wolverhampton was my home and I wanted to stay there. India was a foreign country, where I was sure I would feel out of place.

After the wedding I discovered his visitor's visa was due to run out soon and he would need to become a British citizen to stay here. I did not think it would cause any problems because I was a British citizen born in the country, and a British citizen is allowed to bring her husband here, so it was just a matter of signing the necessary papers. It seemed so straightforward I did not even bother to tell my parents.

Then they refused his application, as they said the primary purpose of the marriage was to stay in this country, to gain settlement. We appealed to the adjudicator. We lost that as well. I still did not really understand anything; I was just learning. I was still not sure what immigration was; I thought that only Black people were immigrants. Gradually I learnt we were really stuck with a problem. When the deportation notice came it really scared us, then I realised that they did not mean to let him stay.

I had always thought of myself as a British girl. That had been one of the problems with my parents: they wanted us all to be good Indian daughters, while we saw ourselves as typically British. At school I had hardly been aware of my colour or of being different because there were so many of us from a variety of backgrounds. I began to understand that my parents were right, it was naive to think of myself as if I was as British as a white girl, because the people in power certainly did not think of me like that. I was beginning to learn about politics.

I had already had my first daughter, Jaquelina, and I felt if I just let Som go back it would be a terrible burden on the child and me. If it had just been me, without a child, I would have sent him back to India to apply from there. But he was a father, and anyway I was pregnant again, expecting my second baby.

I felt the best thing to do was to start a campaign. We wrote to all the advice centres and community centres and we just kept on getting different information. With all the different advice we just did not know who we could trust. For three weeks we hardly slept, as we just did not know what to do. Then a worker at a nearby community centre said she would write a letter to a man called Idrish, who won his campaign after five years. When he replied he suggested that we should go to see him to discuss a campaign. He told us about the problems we would have to deal with, but also how he had managed to win. He gave us three weeks to think about it, but he had talked us into it. We realised that if we just went through the legal process there was no way we could win. The law was so racist: it was about keeping Black people out.

So we decided to start a campaign. I wanted to keep my name out of it – I did not want to be in the paper or on television – and just keep it to Som. The first job was to produce a leaflet and then it just took off. Lots of people supported our campaign: churches, MPs, Som's union, the National Union of Journalists. Suddenly there were lots of speeches to be made as people wanted to make our case known.

There was a lot of pressure on Som and me, because of trying to do all the work and juggling the kids around it. By that time Angelina, our second daughter, had been born. Som started taking me to meetings and conferences where he was speaking, but at first I was too shy to do anything myself.

When I saw how many other people made speeches I thought that if they could do it I could, and after about a year I made myself start doing it too. I just told people the problems we were facing, and how as I was a British citizen I should be able to keep my husband here. I used to tell people about all the pressure we were going through, leaving the kids behind and not seeing enough of them, so they knew how important it was to us. By the end I was speaking at meetings, conferences, rallies and demonstrations, and just being able to do that gave me more confidence that we would win.

From the beginning of the campaign I was convinced we were going to win. Over and over again we would meet other people either in our position or who had already won. I felt we had proved that the primary purpose of the marriage was love because we were still together and had two children. I just did not understand why they would not let Som stay. What used to make me so angry was that the law people would not believe him, although he was telling the truth, while liars were getting away with it. I refused to let it all affect us. Som was really cool all the time and although I got really hot sometimes I just thought if he was cool so should I be. That was how we kept it from affecting our marriage.

The worst bit was sitting in the court in London waiting for the final result. It took the judge over an hour to read out the finding and then announce the result. I was so anxious to listen to it that when it was announced I was not sure I had heard the right thing, I just sat there and sweated. I had been listening so hard I had not understood what she had been saying, I was just hearing unconnected words and phrases. Then everybody got up smiling and started shaking hands and I knew we had won. It took me a couple of days to realise it was real.

I look back on how marrying Som changed my life and I cannot believe in that shy seventeen year-old. At school it was so bad that if I was late for a lesson I would push my friend in first. Now I am not really bothered about anything. I feel I could go out in front of 65 million people and speak.

# MELANIE McFADYEAN

## Out of the Cocoon

*Melanie McFadyean was born in London in 1950. Her schooling was varied, from the abysmal to the wonderful. She left at sixteen and went to university in Leeds, where she studied English literature and got a BA and an MA. There followed a series of jobs, primarily as a waitress. In 1974 she started teaching art in a secondary school in Hackney, London. Two years later she went to Hackney College of Further Education, where she taught English until 1984. In 1980 she cut her teaching to part-time and started freelance journalism. She worked on* Kicks, *a teenage magazine, as fiction editor, advice columnist and feature writer. She worked in Northern Ireland with two co-authors and with them wrote* Only the Rivers Run Free: Northern Ireland, The Women's War. *In 1984 she co-authored* Thatcher's Reign: A Bad Case of the Blues. *That year she started writing* Just Seventeen's *advice pages, which she did until 1988. In 1987 she published her short stories,* Hotel Romantika. *She has written for several publications, among them the* Guardian, *the* Observer, New Society, The New Statesman, The Sunday Times Magazine, The Mail on Sunday. *She is currently working at the* Guardian *as editor of the Young Guardian page.*

## Face powder and the world of women

A Central European visitor drew me aside into the dimness of the winter twilit sitting room and, tilting her face towards the French windows, said, 'Look at me'. I looked. Her skin was yellow, lined and leathery, her expression sad. 'Never wear face powder,' she said seriously, 'or, like me, nobody will ever marry you.' I can still see her face lit by the dwindling light, silhouetted by the dark curtains. I accepted her invitation to look out of curiosity. It was one of those moments that sinks into the consciousness and stays there. It was part of my initiation into the conventions of what goes by the name of female beauty, and the implications of that, handed down from one generation of women to another. (I have never worn face powder.)

## Caliban

An artist came to lunch at school. He had a powerful presence, exciting in me a mixture of thrill, anticipation and acute embarrassment, a young girl's subconscious response to the great darkness of undiscovered sexuality. I don't remember his features, only how dark he was and the look in his eyes – sexy, fiery, full of an energy I recognised but couldn't have named. I was embarrassed because I was sure someone would read my mind and condemn me, for what I wasn't sure.

He looked from one girl to the next, guessing who was playing what part in the end-of-term play, *The Tempest*. He started with the pretty girls, the slim, blonde ones I envied. Looking at me, he said, 'And you, are you Caliban?' His question went to the heart of my confused, innocent, awakening sexuality and left an injury there which partly determined the subsequent course of a chaos from which I sometimes wonder if I have ever recovered.

Caliban, son of the witch Sycorax, is much maligned and maltreated by the shipwrecked magician/philosopher Prospero and his beautiful daughter Miranda, who colonise an island rightfully belonging to Caliban. He is described as 'hag seed', referred to as 'savage'. He is 'not honoured with human shape'. Somebody stumbles across him and holds his nose, saying, 'What have we here, man or fish? He smells like a fish; a very ancient and fish-like smell.' I had in fact been offered the part and had turned it down, not wanting to be seen as remotely

*17*

resembling Caliban. The artist's question confirmed my worst fears. I was a monster and sure that men would always regard me as one, as someone 'not honoured with human shape'.

## Disasters happen to other people
..............................................

Disasters are fascinating. The goriest headline is almost always the most irresistible.

This headline was about an air crash. I looked closely and furtively at the grey and white aerial photographs of the wreckage strewn across expanses of snow, and at the rock face into which the aeroplane had crashed. Perhaps there are lots of people who scrutinise such photographs hoping and dreading that they might see a piece of a limb or a severed head. I thought I was one of some secretive, sick minority who couldn't help themselves, but had to look at such things. I had a creepy feeling that someone would catch me and condemn me for my ghoulish interest. I was also sure that disasters happen only to other people and never to anyone I might know.

I went on poring over the pictures. One was of a young girl laughing. She looked familiar. I looked again. It was someone I'd been to school with. Twenty-three years later I can remember her, although I didn't know her well. She was an attractive, popular, vivacious girl. And she was dead. Life hangs on a finer thread than I knew until then. Disasters and tragedies happen to people – not other people.

There was a girl at another school I went to later. She was a wild, loud, funny girl. The expression in her eyes was unusual in someone of sixteen. Something resigned? Flat? Her reputation went before her and she was expected to be larger than life, but life turned out to be larger than her. She committed suicide.

Death lends a glamour and vividness even to people one hardly knew or maybe never even met. Dead people linger in the consciousness, but had they lived some of them might have passed by, leaving no trace.

## The real world

In the era of my boarding-school days we were allowed to watch very little television, and radio listening was heavily censored. Those were the days of the ink pen and lessons in deportment. Biros were bad for handwriting and girls who couldn't stand up straight were no asset to anyone. Pop music corrupted the morals and television rotted the brain. But at my last school, a concession was won from the teachers by a continued assault on their patience. They decided we could watch television once a week for two hours. They let us see 'The Man from UNCLE' and 'Top of the Pops'. The result was that the collective dirty dream was most often about Ilya Kuriakin, the small hero of 'Man from UNCLE'.

But we were allowed to read Sunday newspapers, even encouraged to do so. It was the mid 1960s, the time of the Vietnam War. Sunday brought the real world into the confines of a Wiltshire girls' boarding school. There were haunting photographs of the Vietnamese people under fire from the Americans and their allies. The ones that had the most impact were of children running naked and crying in pain and terror, their little bodies scorched by napalm.

## PPS I love you

One summer I developed a love of minor forms of arson. I would walk along country lanes at weekends during the summer term at school, throwing lighted matches into the hedgerows. Small fires would start. It must have been a damp summer because nothing ever flared up. During one such arson stroll I met some boys from the 'brother' school. I can't remember how we got talking, but the main thing was, one boy singled me out and held my hand. He did this in front of other girls and boys, which meant that other people saw that I was the object of a boy's desire. It didn't matter what his personality was like, he was holding my hand. The monster was having its hand held.

During the summer holidays he wrote me several letters on dark blue paper with matching envelopes. He had cramped, awkward, backward-sloping handwriting. For some reason this seemed a bad sign, but I overlooked it. (Such generosity.)

He lived in Formby, Lancashire and I in Puddletown, Dorset. I kept his letters and recently came across them. In the first letter he wishes he could be 'down south' with me. He wants to share my troubles and is sorry I'm going through them alone. (I must have sent him the unexpurgated, unofficial, private version of the complexity and drama of my family life.) He says he has troubles of his own: 'Two days ago my mother went out and bought a puppy (Yorkshire terrier) ever since then it has been plaguing me. It even sleeps on my pillow.' I wasn't impressed by his 'troubles'. My mother tells me I used to stage suicide attempts in the River Piddle, which ran through our garden. There I was face down in the weeds and waters of the River Piddle, attempting to meet my Maker, while he was worrying about the affections of a Yorkshire terrier. The pillock. But I forgave him and overlooked this as well as the handwriting, because on the next page were just three words – 'I miss you.' The last traces of scorn vanished as I got to the end of the letter: 'PS I am growing fond of you.'

Every letter evoked this curious duality of scorn and adoration. In the next he describes a trip to London, staying at the Hilton and 'buying everything I could possibly need within the next few years'. I didn't like that either, such acquisitiveness wasn't romantic. Love ebbed with each line. But again, as the letter drew to a close, all was forgiven: 'I must see you sometime when you don't have to dive into a bush every time a car appears. The heart grows fonder in absence may as is a very true fact, I for one can vouch for this but I feel there must be a limit or I shall go —. To me you are the sweetest girl in the world, and I wish I could say that to your face.' (Please note the grammar and so on; it is of significance later.) 'I am longing to see you,' he continues, 'and in the meantime I will have to dream about you instead.' Heaven and bliss, blushes and hot flushes over breakfast, and savoured again and again the second post script: 'PPS I love you'. (On one level I thought him silly and dull, but on the other he had said he loved me. This released me, temporarily and spasmodically, from being Caliban.')

I never saw him again. Something went terribly wrong, I can't remember what. His last letter is cold and angry: 'I am returning your letter for want of anything better to do with it. It is the worst load of rubbish I have ever encountered and have had my fair share. This may come as a surprise to you, but your admirers' opinions of you are considerably lower than vice versa. You're feelings are not the only things which are not very stable and solid, your grammar isn't so hot either. As to your request concerning the goings on in my "seething little mind" – from this point on nothing to do with you.'

Oh dear. This episode confirmed that boys were both God and pillock. They were to be worshipped, adored and revered one moment, and the next regarded with pity, contempt or scorn. It was taken for granted that girls were warm, entertaining, funny and communicative, but when a boy showed warmth, wit or depth, it was a bonus.

Boys weren't our equals. They were simultaneously superior and inferior. They had to be impressed, their interest culled by a canny mixture of distance and veiled availability, but somehow they were also to be humoured and understood. If a girl betrayed or hurt another the fight could be bitter, the abuse hurled, and sometimes there would be fists and hair-pulling, but all could be forgiven and ranks would once more close. But once a boy had fallen from grace, he was beyond mercy. I wonder why this was. Perhaps it was early intimations of the balance of power. From girls we expected integrity. From boys we expected difficulty, harassment, heartache, rejection or pain. Perhaps it's part of an inheritance of that old war between men and women. It's sad that it starts so young.

## The badness of adults

'Now that I have become a man I have put away childish things,' a quotation from the Bible often read at school prayers. We used to laugh when it was read because we weren't going to become 'men'. Perhaps part of the trouble with adults is that they put away childish things. Some childish things would be best held on to – spontaneity, instinct, honesty, curiosity, zest, imagination. It wasn't until I became an adult that I saw adults aren't a wiser species. They're just bigger, they're the people with the keys and the power.

I began to know this without consciously seeing it when I was sixteen and expelled from school.

The headmistress was a weird, bloodless sort of woman. I was very wayward but managed not to get caught. She wanted to catch me but had failed. Her vigilance was wearing me down and I offered her a deal. I promised to tell her all the naughty things I'd done and to go straight until A levels were over, in exchange for a punishment that would not involve my parents. I asked her not to expel me as my mother's second marriage was on the point of collapse and I didn't want to add to her burdens. The headmistress agreed not to tell my parents and not to expel me.

I told her everything from the most exotic to the most trivial. I told her that I had been one of the two girls smuggled to the boys' school in the boot of a bus during a heat wave. I said we'd stripped to the waist and opened the doors to empty the bucket we'd peed in. The man in the Morris Traveller behind must have been the one who reported us. I confessed that the poetry I produced on my return from the woods had not taken all weekend of agony to write but was dashed off in a few minutes, and that I spent some of my weekends rambling around the countryside in a very old car with a friend who'd been expelled from his school. She assumed we were having wild sex, so I put her straight on that: we were pals and never so much as held hands. I don't suppose she believed me.

She wanted to know what the progress was with the play I was writing at the boys' school based on the lives of Robert Browning and Elizabeth Barrett. I admitted there'd never really been any play and agreed that it had been a waste of school time and money hiring the period costume that I wore every week for the play-writing sessions. What had we in fact been doing, she asked. I expect she thought again that I'd been having wild sex, but again I put her straight. We'd been drinking. They had a crate of whisky stolen from an alcoholic schoolmaster who couldn't report them without showing himself up. The only lie I told was that I said it was wine, I don't know why. I went into some detail over each story, and in this particular one I told her that there was one evening when a boy with very big hands put one of his very big hands on one of my bosoms. I told her about the naked bacchanalian rituals in the school chapel when for a lark we sacrificed one of our gang on the altar, drunk on Cinzano smuggled into the school. The list of offences went on and on.

A few weeks went by and she didn't appear to have decided on my punishment. She treated me like anyone else. This was ominous. One Sunday I went to the school phone box and tapped my father's number. (I didn't tell her about tapping the phone because that would have spoiled it for all the other girls.) After some tense moments of silence, my father spoke: 'I'm meeting you on the four o'clock at Waterloo.' I was about to be expelled, and I was the last one to know it.

I burst into the headmistress's study, swearing without restraint. She had prospective parents with her. They looked terrified, which gave me both courage and pleasure. She stood in front of them as though to protect them from a wild circus animal on the loose, saying under her breath that I came from a 'broken home' and an 'artistic background'. Artistic background, broken home, so what, I shouted at her. She edged the horrified couple out of the room and gestured to me to sit down. I complied; I was running out of steam, beginning to see the size of the situation, and feeling increasingly unhappy.

Looking at me pleadingly, she went on her knees and said she'd had to do it for the sake of the younger girls who were being influenced by me. This silenced and horrified me. What had I done to younger girls? It hardly mattered whether that was her real reason or not, and I don't think it was. She was canny and must have known that would hurt and disturb me.

From then on I knew, without being able to articulate it, that there are adults in positions of power who abuse that power: who lie, break their word, behave far worse than the children they'd be the first to punish for far lesser crimes.

## Mexico City 1967

It was the rainy season in Mexico and every day, from four o'clock to seven o'clock, the rain came down. It was heavy, tropical rain, unlike English rain, and I loved it, revelling in its excess and the moods it invoked – sometimes melancholy, sometimes wildly excited. One such rainy evening, I returned to the city after a trip to Popacatapetl mountain. I was with an Irishman who had befriended me, and a couple he knew. They were twice my age at least; I was sixteen. I had met the man when we were both locked into the anthropological museum on another rainy afternoon, hidden from each other in the shadows of huge Aztec sculptures. He had emerged into the dimness of the gallery, silhouetted against the plate glass that stretched from floor to ceiling, beyond which were enormous metasequoia trees with rusty-coloured bark and dark branches. He did not frighten me.

For several weeks we visited markets and ziggurats and backstreets. We were friends, companions. There was no hint of romance or sex, and I felt safe with him.

On the evening when we came back from Popacatapetl, the rain was falling heavily as usual. We got out of his friend's old Chevrolet and ran through the garden into the house. My dress was soaked and sticking to me by the time we got to the door. He suggested I put it on the radiator and wrap myself in a towel until it dried out. I wasn't worried and did as he suggested. I came out of the bathroom and sat, wrapped in the towel, on the edge of the sofa bed, shivering slightly and by then feeling a little awkward. I must have been looking down because I remember looking up and at my eye level was a penis. It gave me a real fright. I'd never been told that penises grow.

I ran to the bathroom and put my wet dress back on. Then I ran straight out of the house, through the garden and into the street. He caught up with me, apologising and looking sincerely desperate. I hailed a passing cab and as I got into it he managed to shut the door on my hand. It was a confusing moment. The taxi drove away as I winced with the pain of my crushed hand.

Years later I was walking along a crowded London street. He was walking towards me. I recognised him instantly. As we passed, I looked him in the eye. He returned my look without a flicker of recognition.

If a sixteen-year-old girl told me this had happened to her, I would be angry with the man for losing control. I would imagine she had somehow been psychologically damaged. Perhaps I would put the idea into her head that somehow she should feel damaged. But I don't think I was. I was frightened because nobody had ever explained that penises grow like that. And I resent his inability to control his urges. I never told anyone what had happened, aware that I would be blamed – people would say, you were there, you should have known better. I didn't feel angry then, nor do I now in retrospect, just sad that my innocence was tampered with and glad that I ran.

## A bizarre procedure

My younger brother was about eight when our stepfather told him the facts of life. He was sitting in the bath playing with boats and a clockwork dolphin. My stepfather carefully explained. My brother pondered momentarily while whirring the dolphin's flappers, then said, 'What a bizarre procedure.' Where an eight-year-old got the phrase from remains a mystery, but I knew what he meant.

I was a wild teenager, but sex wasn't prominent on my agenda. Romance was. My fantasies were in the realm of meaningful moments and the understanding and unplumbable depths of perfect communication between me and the mythical Other. The physical side of the fantasies was confined to screen-style kisses, wooing and loving, billing and cooing, all pretty clean.

Thanks to the version of the 'Colonel Bogey' tune I knew, I thought all men had different numbers of balls: 'Hitler has only got one ball, Goebbels has got no balls at all.' I assumed that good men, in contrast to bad men like Hitler and Goebbels, would be awarded with a greater number of balls hanging from them like bunches of plums.

I was eighteen and independent, living in an attic in Leeds for £1 a week and studying at the university. It's odd now to think how little I knew about all sorts of things. I had no idea how to look after myself and lived on digestive biscuits, chips and chop suey rolls. I smoked cigarettes because I wanted to be like the women they used in tobacco advertisements in those days – long, elegant, successful women, seen to be desired. And then I met a very nice young man a few years older than me. He was funny and friendly and a bit eccentric. We became friends. The friendship shifted ground one Sunday when I contrived, with a little help from the Leeds City Corporation, to miss the last bus home. He chivalrously offered me his bed and I accepted, having already decided I wanted to lose my virginity. Losing your virginity, I and several million virgins throughout history had been led to believe, was a very big deal. If my experience was a big deal, it was because I found it a bizarre procedure. I had always imagined, in so far as I'd got beyond the screen kiss in my fantasies, that the man and woman lie on their sides looking into each other's eyes. Then the man puts his penis into the woman and something spectacular happens. I imagined he'd say wonderful things and we'd fall asleep in each other's arms.

In the event, the experience bore no resemblance to screen romance or to the descriptions I'd read in books. (There were always books wrapped in brown paper which circulated at school with the 'good' bits easily identifiable by their well-thumbed, dog-eared pages.)

But I still felt proud afterwards; I felt I was a woman and not a girl. I kept quiet about the discovery that forbidden fruit doesn't necessarily taste very spectacular, and revelled in the knowing looks of the other girls when I conveyed to them, in deliberately half-formed sentences and smiles I pretended to suppress, that I had done that momentous thing. And I looked with less awe at the adult world which had, yet again, misled me. All those books and films and magazines, those poems and songs, the laughter and whispering in corners, all that promise and confusion – amidst it nobody managed to whisper that sex could just be a rather ordinary – if bizarre – procedure the first time. (And what a revelation to discover that balls come in twos and not in indeterminate bunches.)

## Out of the cocoon

There were three of us sitting around a coal fire, chatting amicably. We were all about eighteen and at university. The girl and I were talking about art. It seemed an ordinary sort of conversation to me. The young man, who I thought I knew so well, fell silent. The atmosphere became tense, the way it can when one in a group of three withdraws. Suddenly, without any comment, he stormed out of the room.

I felt embarrassed, as though his exit were my fault. The girl and I looked at each other, bewildered and uneasy. I withdrew into my cocoon, looking for comfort, but found none. At some level I understood his anger, but I couldn't explain it then.

The girl and I shared an unquestioning certainty that the world and its treasures were ours. We had had expensive educations and had absorbed a culture and an identity from which, I see now, he felt in some ways excluded. Art, music, foreign languages, self-confidence and sure-footedness were ours. We took it for granted that we would have charmed and interesting lives. We were born into a class which ensured us ease of passage which could be interrupted only by accidents of fate – or so it seemed to me at the time.

A few weeks after he had stormed out of that room, the young man took me home to meet his family. His widowed mother lived in a small house on an estate in an east coast seaside town. She lived with her old mother, who rambled and chattered constantly. There was no luxury, nothing valuable, none of the objects which adorned the variety of houses inhabited by my fragmented family. It's a very English thing that the language of common rituals marks one class from another. They had dinner at one; we had lunch. They had tea at five, a proper meal; we had a cup of tea at four and dinner at eight. His mother had never been abroad and spoke no foreign languages. My parents had travelled widely, often taking us with them, and spoke at least two languages each. His mother worked as a cleaner in a local hospital; in our family someone came in to do the cleaning.

Luckily for him and me, neither family created any awkwardness for us, and wherever we were there was warmth.

When he so angrily left that fireside, the cocoon I had inhabited lost some of its innocent, ignorant protection. Out of it, and beyond its muffled chrysalis, were other lives.

I see a group of people. They are looking at each other with interest and suspicion. They are a funny, disparate group, wondering what the connections between them are. They are as if in a dream.

Among them are the Central European visitor, the artist with his hot eyes, Caliban, the girls who died, Vietnamese children burned by napalm. There is the boyfriend absurd in cape and monocle with the tedious terrier in tow. There is Ilya Kuriakin and pop stars with forgotten names. There are groups of schoolgirls, all elbows and laughter. The man in the Morris Traveller looks ahead, shocked. Petrified parents shrink in fear behind the headmistress in her disguise of wisdom and authority, and my little brother sits in a bath playing with his clockwork dolphin. My stepfather regards him with amusement. The Irishman is there, and so are the Aztec sculptures; the young man from the seaside town and his mother and grandmother look on. My parents speak to each other in foreign languages.

I watch or am being watched. I am inside and outside, threading my way through the people, hearing a kind of murmuring. I am Caliban, I am wearing an Elizabeth Barrett Browning costume or a summer dress wet with Mexican rain. I am fat, sad and lonely and then suddenly larking about in abandon. I try to learn the languages of adults, always imagining their world is somewhere I will one day arrive in without really noticing.

The past sometimes looks like that. The moments and experiences that leave traces don't always feel special at the time. Some sink like silent implosions. They are like faults in subterranean rock faces, perhaps causing an earthquake years and years after they appear. They are like waves which have an ocean to cross before breaking on the shore. Perhaps they don't deserve poetic images, perhaps they are like rubbish left at the bottom of a garden that gradually rots down into something that can help the garden to grow.

# SHREELA GHOSH

## *She's Leaving Home*

I *was born in Shillong, a hill station in the foothills of the Himalayas, in India. My father left to come to England when I was four and we were reunited as a family seven years later when my mother, brother and I came to England. Three years later the three of us left for India again, so my childhood was split between India and England. My formal education stopped at sixteen and I did a variety of jobs until becoming an actress, then landed the part of Naima in 'EastEnders'. I have now left that and live in north London with my husband and two children.*

*I must emphasise that this is my story, not every Asian woman's. It is a particular family history and my peculiar relationship with my father is not a typical Asian experience – it is just mine.*

In February 1977, at the age of fourteen, I came to Britain to live with my father, leaving my mother and brother back in Calcutta. My future was mapped out: I would finish my schooling and go on to university. My parents were both academics, so Oxford or Cambridge was expected. My mother was torn between her dream of seeing me do a ward round in a white coat with a stethoscope round my neck or respectfully addressing me as Vice-Chancellor of Calcutta University. Parallel to my brilliant career would be a 'match-made-in-heaven'-type marriage: they would not have to force me to marry anyone but would gently persuade me to pick one of the eligible bachelors on offer. My parents could not have fixed a proper arranged marriage, as their own was rumoured to have been a legendary love match.

To my great relief, in August 1978 my parents' love match

finally disintegrated. The play-acting of family life could stop. It left my mother shattered, her life in pieces; it gave my father licence to carry on debauching in peace. They made a pact to live on opposite sides of the globe: the only way of guaranteeing that my mother's life would not be in danger. I have one wonderful memory of my father tenderly kissing my mother, but many haunting images of him violently throttling, punching or kicking her.

I was sixteen when my parents separated, and I chose to continue to live in England with my father. The deal was that I should finish off my O levels and then do A levels.

I found living with my father extremely difficult. My middle-class Bengali background, combined with my idolisation of my father and his Marxist rhetoric, had not prepared me for how he intended to live his life. Suddenly I found myself having to share the family home with the various women he was having relationships with.

My father had agreed to let me come back to England as long as I would be absolutely no trouble to him. The conditions were firmly laid down: along with the one-way plane ticket from Calcutta he sent me a contract like the Ten Commandments, which had to be obeyed. Basically, unlike most teenagers, I was not allowed to go out. I was not even allowed to speak to my friends on the telephone after school, as there was a lock on it.

I found it very unfair that where he could elucidate at length about oppression and exploitation on a global scale, on the home front he seemed oblivious to it. He lived this very liberated life, yet I was a virtual prisoner. I found it difficult to mix with people at school because I could not see them outside, but I did make a few very good friends, whose support I needed at the time.

Luckily I had a sensitive class tutor who picked up on my stressful domestic situation, and we got very close and talked. When she asked me what I wanted to do, all I could think about was staying on at school after my O levels. I had been brought up in such a straitjacket that school was my only sanctuary. I did not want to leave, but I did not want to live at home. I just had to get out of home. She tried to help me find a way of doing that, but it was impossible.

If you want to stay at school you either live at home or get taken into care. There is no way of independently living out; the system just does not deal with it. My teacher put me in touch with social workers and I decided I did not want to get taken into care. The only other option I could see was to go to night school part-time and get a job during the day.

My father was away for six weeks in America that summer, and I knew it was my opportunity to cut loose. I left a letter for him and kept a copy:

Dear Ba
Thank you for the postcard which you sent me. I hope you had a good holiday.

Before you went away you remember we had a few discussions about the future and you gave me a choice of staying with you on your terms or going for good. At the time it seemed to me it would be best for both of us if I stayed, but during the last month I have thought about it a lot and it now seems that it would be better for me to go so that you can be freer and not have the constant worry of supporting me.

I have left you a copy of the letter I have written to Mr Kelly and you will see that I have got things sorted out for myself. At the moment I don't want to give you my address because I want you to have time to get used to things.

I am all right so please don't worry or do anything silly like go to the police or anything. I will be in touch with you regularly by post to let you know how I am getting on. I have told Ma of my decision and I shall continue to write to her as usual. Perhaps in a few months we could see each other again. I have left the £20 (for emergencies) with this note. Thank you for leaving it with me. I have also left the key. Don't bother to find me because I have not told anyone my address.

I hope you will write and let me know how you are. It would be nice if we could stay friends. I do hope that you will see why I have done what seems to be something dramatic, but what in fact was the only way I could see of making life better for both of us.

Shona

In 1978, being sixteen, reasonably smart and armed with eight O levels, finding a job was easier than finding somewhere to live. I walked into the London Art Bookshop (just off Kensington Church Street) one Saturday afternoon to enquire if they needed anyone. Little did I know that the man behind the counter was Andreas Papadakis, who had a little publishing empire. The following Monday I was grappling with a doll's eye switchboard and frequently cutting off calls to Paris, New York or Berlin. I was paid the enormous sum of £60 a week and I thought I had arrived.

After a few weeks of scouting the *Evening Standard*'s flatshare pages and travelling from Ealing to Leytonstone in search of accommodation, I finally twigged that it was my age which was putting people off. Landlords were sceptical about harbouring runaway Asian girls; prospective flatmates were less than enthusiastic about sharing with a naive teenager.

Meanwhile, time was running out. My father was due back from America.

I took my suitcase full of clothes and three cardboard boxes full of books and other belongings, boarded the Number 102 bus, and with the help of my mate Masher moved into a Working Woman's Hostel in Muswell Hill. In India Working Woman's Hostels are respectable – akin to YWCAs here. My expectations were to be dashed in the first twenty-four hours. Miss Curran, the warden, explained the rules: there was an

11 p.m. curfew, I was to share a room with two other girls, and the weekly rate was £11. I moved my boxes into my corner of the room and met one of my room mates, who was a single parent on anti-depressants. The other girl I was to meet later that night when, having clambered up the drainpipe, she squeezed herself in through the bathroom window to evade the curfew. The next morning I asked Curran why there were no bath plugs, only to be told one had to have one's own because they kept getting nicked.

I lasted a week at 11 Princess Avenue – any longer and I think I would have needed anti-depressants too. On Saturday morning a blue Mini parked outside the door and out stepped my knight in shining armour and carried me, my boxes and my suitcase half a mile down the road to Cranley Gardens. What luxury to be given a properly furnished room all to myself, use of living room, bathroom (complete with plug), kitchen and garden – all for £25 a week.

I got in touch with all the Further Education colleges where I could take A levels at night school, and chose the Working Men's College in Camden. I started off with good intentions to work hard. I enrolled to do politics, history and sociology, which was bloody ambitious as I was doing it only part-time, but three A levels was what all my friends were doing, so I just thought it was the thing to do. By Christmas I had dropped sociology because it was boring and taken up law, and by Easter I had dropped law because I found it too difficult, and by the summer I ended just taking one, which was history.

Simon, my knight in the Mini, was the son of a friend of a friend. He was in his early twenties, good-looking, and I had a crush on him. I made a trip to the family doctor to ask for the pill and was pleasantly surprised not to be given any hassle. I was not a virgin. (One of my teachers, a fellow Marxist friend of my father's, had seen to that. Now I know it was rape, but at the time I was too confused to understand it was not my fault.)

However, Simon and his friends were to initiate me into the world of sex. At the same time I was to discover drugs and booze too. I had tasted wine at home – when my father had friends over to dinner I would be given a drop sometimes. I had even mixed the odd gin and tonic (three-quarters gin, one quarter tonic was my recipe) and almost killed our visitors, but I had never seen the inside of a pub until I became a regular at the Royal Oak. Our evening would start at the Oak (famous for its relaxed attitude to underage drinking), then we would get a cab to the West End clubs, smoke a joint or two *en route* and pop a few pills. Some hours later I would be back in bed at Cranley Gardens with Tom, Dick or Harry.

Over the few months I stayed there I changed both mentally and physically. I left behind my school friends, most of whom had stayed on to do A levels: I was moving in an adult world; they were mere children.

I had only just discovered the world of work, and having my own money which I could spend as I wanted, over the past month. It may sound ridiculous, but at the age of seventeen I had never bought my own clothes; they were always bought by my father because he was afraid I would squander money. So all my clothes had been very straight, like checked shirts and hideous coats; almost everything was shapeless, and all the shoes were flat. There were two things which I would wear when I saw my friends, things that I thought were cool. One was a pair of dungarees which were really big and baggy; I forget the brand name but do remember it was trendy. (I went to my first Rock Against Racism concert wearing those dungarees!) The other was a pair of navy cords. What I used to do, however, was borrow his clothes. He may have locked the telephone but he did not lock his wardrobe and he had – in fact still has – a superb collection of Italian jumpers, which his Italian woman sent every Christmas, and quite often if ever I had the opportunity to go out – and it was usually while he was out of the country on one of his holidays – I would nick one of those jumpers because they really were nice.

It was wonderful working for Academy Editions in Kensington because there are such lovely shops round there. Finally I could buy clothes which I thought suited and flattered me, clothes I wanted.

I became increasingly unreliable at work and in a fit of pique walked out of the job one day. The following week I started answering telephones at another publishing firm near Muswell Hill. I needed to earn to pay my rent and keep my new-found friends happy. They had begun to ask me to pay for the cabs into town and buy the drinks at the pubs and clubs. I found myself living on pork pies and the odd bag of chips. Constantly taking speed, I was not hungry most of the time.

I liked what was happening to my body. I had never been fat but now I was beginning to look really slim – the most important thing in the world to me was to be desired by the guys at Cranley Gardens. It did not matter that I derived no actual pleasure from sex: as long as they wanted to do it and seemed to enjoy it, I was happy. It was to be another couple of years before I was aware that sex could be more than just satisfying men.

It was illness that woke me from this reverie. Those months of abuse were a total shock to my body: it gave up on me just as a new decade was about to begin. In January 1980 I developed a high fever with very bad stomach pains. My doctor diagnosed appendicitis and I was taken to hospital. As I lay on the operating table the surgeon decided it was not appendicitis, merely a urinary tract infection. I was saved from an unnecessary operation, but the whole experience scared me enough to start looking after myself.

I began dancing again. Thankfully, the one outlet my father had allowed me was traditional Indian dancing, which I had kept up when I left home. Perhaps it gave me the confidence and discipline to try acting. I had no formal training and I was only seventeen, but I was picked for a BBC Play for Today. My experiences were very similar to the character I was playing: a young Asian girl who leaves home after having problems with her family. This gave me a lot of the strength and insight I needed to play her. It was quite a big part and I'd never worked so hard in my life.

A couple of years later I landed a role in *Jewel in the Crown*. I played Minnie, the Ayah who saves the baby from the ring of fire. Here I was, a virtually untrained actress, watching and learning from really professional actors. Then came another lucky break: I was chosen to play Naima in *EastEnders*. In a soap you work day in and day out with a hundred different directors and writers and you're constantly in front of the cameras. That was a completely different sort of challenge and discipline.

I think I learned a lot by leaving home . . .

# MAYA ANGELOU

......................................

## And Still I Rise

**M**aya Angelou was born in 1928 in St Louis, Missouri. After the
break-up of her parents' marriage she and her beloved brother
Bailey went to live with her grandmother, whose General Store was
the centre of life for the Black community in Stamps, Arkansas.

At eight, she was raped by her mother's boyfriend and for the
next five years she became mute. When she was sixteen, having just
graduated from school, Maya gave birth to her son Guy.

In the years that followed she has been waitress, singer, actress,
dancer, Black activist (working with Martin Luther King),
composer, director, and filmmaker. Her poetry and her five-volume
autobiography, the first of which is I Know Why the Caged Bird
Sings, have made her one of the world's most admired Black
women.

She lives in North Carolina where she is Reynolds Professor at
Wake Forest University.

......................................

The children in Stamps trembled visibly with anticipation.
Some adults were excited too, but to be certain the whole young
population had come down with graduation epidemic. Large
classes were graduating from both the grammar school and the
high school. Even those who were years removed from their
own day of glorious release were anxious to help with preparations as a kind of dry run. The junior students who were
moving into the vacating classes' chairs were tradition-bound to
show their talents for leadership and management. They strutted
through the school and around the campus exerting pressure on
the lower grades. Their authority was so new that occasionally
if they pressed a little too hard it had to be overlooked. After
all, next term was coming, and it never hurt a sixth grader to

have a play sister in the eighth grade, or a tenth-year student to be able to call a twelfth grader Bubba. So all was endured in a spirit of shared understanding. But the graduating classes themselves were the nobility. Like travelers with exotic destinations on their minds, the graduates were remarkably forgetful. They came to school without their books, or tablets or even pencils. Volunteers fell over themselves to secure replacements for the missing equipment. When accepted, the willing workers might or might not be thanked, and it was of no importance to the pregraduation rites. Even teachers were respectful of the now quiet and aging seniors, and tended to speak to them, if not as equals, as beings only slightly lower than themselves. After tests were returned and grades given, the student body, which acted like an extended family, knew who did well, who excelled, and what piteous ones had failed.

Unlike the white high school, Lafayette County Training School distinguished itself by having neither lawn, nor hedges, nor tennis court, nor climbing ivy. Its two buildings (main classrooms, the grade school and home economics) were set on a dirt hill with no fence to limit either its boundaries or those of bordering farms. There was a large expanse to the left of the school which was used alternately as a baseball diamond or a basketball court. Rusty hoops on the swaying poles represented the permanent recreational equipment, although bats and balls could be borrowed from the PE teacher if the borrower was qualified and if the diamond wasn't occupied.

Over this rocky area relieved by a few shady tall persimmon trees the graduating class walked. The girls often held hands and no longer bothered to speak to the lower students. There was a sadness about them, as if this old world was not their home and they were bound for higher ground. The boys, on the other hand, had become more friendly, more outgoing. A decided change from the closed attitude they projected while studying for finals. Now they seemed not ready to give up the old school, the familiar paths and classrooms. Only a small percentage would be continuing on to college – one of the South's A & M (agricultural and mechanical) schools, which trained Negro youths to be carpenters, farmers, handymen, masons, maids, cooks and baby nurses. Their future rode heavily on their shoulders, and blinded them to the collective joy that had pervaded the lives of the boys and girls in the grammar school graduating class.

Parents who could afford it had ordered new shoes and ready-made clothes for themselves from Sears and Roebuck or Montgomery Ward. They also engaged the best seamstresses to make the floating graduating dresses and to cut down secondhand pants which would be pressed to a military slickness for the important event.

Oh, it was important, all right. Whitefolks would attend the ceremony, and two or three would speak of God and home, and the Southern way of life, and Mrs Parsons, the principal's wife, would play the graduation march while the lower-grade graduates paraded down the aisles and took their seats below the platform. The high school seniors would wait in empty classrooms to make their dramatic entrance.

In the Store I was the person of the moment. The birthday girl. The center. Bailey had graduated the year before, although to do so he had had to forfeit all pleasures to make up for his time lost in Baton Rouge.

My class was wearing butter-yellow piqué dresses, and Momma launched out on mine. She smocked the yoke into tiny crisscrossing puckers, then shirred the rest of the bodice. Her dark fingers ducked in and out of the lemony cloth as she embroidered raised daisies around the hem. Before she considered herself finished she had added a crocheted cuff on the puff sleeves, and a pointy crocheted collar.

I was going to be lovely. A walking model of all the various styles of fine hand sewing and it didn't worry me that I was only twelve years old and merely graduating from the eighth grade.

Besides, many teachers in Arkansas Negro schools had only that diploma and were licensed to impart wisdom.

The days had become longer and more noticeable. The faded beige of former times had been replaced with strong and sure colors. I began to see my classmates' clothes, their skin tones, and the dust that waved off pussy willows. Clouds that lazed across the sky were objects of great concern to me. Their shiftier shapes might have held a message that in my new happiness and with a little bit of time I'd soon decipher. During that period I looked at the arch of heaven so religiously my neck kept a steady ache. I had taken to smiling more often, and my jaws hurt from the unaccustomed activity. Between the two physical sore spots, I suppose I could have been uncomfortable, but that was not the case. As a member of the winning team (the graduating class of 1940) I had outdistanced unpleasant sensations by miles. I was headed for the freedom of open fields.

Youth and social approval allied themselves with me and we trammeled memories of slights and insults. The wind of our swift passage remodeled my features. Lost tears were pounded to mud and then to dust. Years of withdrawal were brushed aside and left behind, as hanging ropes of parasitic moss.

My work alone had awarded me a top place and I was going to be one of the first called in the graduating ceremonies. On the classroom blackboard, as well as on the bulletin board in the auditorium, there were blue stars and white stars and red stars. No absences, no tardinesses, and my academic work was among the best of the year. I could say the preamble to the Constitution even faster than Bailey. We timed ourselves often: 'Wethe peopleoftheUnitedStatesinordertoformamoreperfectunion . . .' I had memorized the Presidents of the United States from Washington to Roosevelt in chronological as well as alphabetical order.

My hair pleased me too. Gradually the black mass had lengthened and thickened, so that it kept at last to its braided pattern, and I didn't have to yank my scalp off when I tried to comb it.

Louise and I had rehearsed the exercises until we tired out ourselves. Henry Reed was class valedictorian. He was a small, very black boy with hooded eyes, a long, broad nose and an oddly shaped head. I had admired him for years because each term he and I vied for the best grades in our class. Most often he bested me, but instead of being disappointed I was pleased that we shared top places between us. Like many Southern Black children, he lived with his grandmother, who was as strict as Momma and as kind as she knew how to be. He was courteous, respectful and soft-spoken to elders, but on the playground he chose to play the roughest games. I admired him. Anyone, I reckoned, sufficiently afraid or sufficiently dull could be polite. But to be able to operate at a top level with both adults and children was admirable.

His valedictory speech was entitled 'To Be or Not to Be'. The rigid tenth-grade teacher had helped him write it. He'd been working on the dramatic stresses for months.

The weeks until graduation were filled with heady activities. A group of small children were to be presented in a play about buttercups and daisies and bunny rabbits. They could be heard throughout the building practicing their hops and their little songs that sounded like silver bells. The older girls (nongraduates, of course) were assigned the task of making refreshments for the night's festivities. A tangy scent of ginger, cinnamon, nutmeg and chocolate wafted around the home economics building as the budding cooks made samples for themselves and their teachers.

In every corner of the workshop, axes and saws split fresh timber as the woodshop boys made sets and stage scenery. Only the graduates were left out of the general bustle. We were free to sit in the library at the back of the building or look in quite detachedly, naturally, on the measures being taken for our event.

Even the minister preached on graduation the Sunday before. His subject was, 'Let your light so shine that men will see your good works and praise your Father, Who is in Heaven.' Although the sermon was purported to be addressed to us, he used the occasion to speak to backsliders, gamblers and general ne'er-do-wells. But since he had called our names at the beginning of the service we were mollified.

Among Negroes the tradition was to give presents to children going only from one grade to another. How much more important this was when the person was graduating at the top of the class. Uncle Willie and Momma had sent away for a Mickey Mouse watch like Bailey's. Louise gave me four embroidered handkerchiefs. (I gave her three crocheted doilies.) Mrs Sneed, the minister's wife, made me an underskirt to wear for graduation, and nearly every customer gave me a nickel or maybe even a dime with the instruction 'Keep on moving to higher ground', or some such encouragement.

Amazingly the great day finally dawned and I was out of bed before I knew it. I threw open the back door to see it more clearly, but Momma said, 'Sister, come away from that door and put your robe on.'

I hoped the memory of that morning would never leave me. Sunlight was itself still young, and the day had none of the insistence maturity would bring it in a few hours. In my robe and barefoot in the backyard, under cover of going to see about my new beans, I gave myself up to the gentle warmth and thanked God that no matter what evil I had done in my life He had allowed me to live to see this day. Somewhere in my fatalism I had expected to die, accidentally, and never have the chance to walk up the stairs in the auditorium and gracefully receive my hard-earned diploma. Out of God's merciful bosom I had won reprieve.

Bailey came out in his robe and gave me a box wrapped in Christmas paper. He said he had saved his money for months to pay for it. It felt like a box of chocolates, but I knew Bailey wouldn't save money to buy candy when we had all we could want under our noses.

He was as proud of the gift as I. It was a soft-leather-bound copy of a collections of poems by Edgar Allan Poe, or, as Bailey and I called him, 'Eap'. I turned to 'Annabel Lee' and we walked up and down the garden rows, the cool dirt between our toes, reciting the beautifully sad lines.

Momma made a Sunday breakfast although it was only Friday. After we finished the blessing, I opened my eyes to find the watch on my plate. It was a dream of a day. Everything went smoothly and to my credit. I didn't have to be reminded or scolded for anything. Near evening I was too jittery to attend to chores, so Bailey volunteered to do all before his bath.

Days before, we had made a sign for the Store, and as we turned out the lights Momma hung the cardboard over the doorknob. It read clearly: CLOSED. GRADUATION.

My dress fitted perfectly and everyone said that I looked like a sunbeam in it. On the hill, going toward the school, Bailey walked behind with Uncle Willie, who muttered, 'Go on, Ju.' He wanted him to walk ahead with us because it embarrassed him to have to walk so slowly. Bailey said he'd let the ladies walk together, and the men would bring up the rear. We all laughed, nicely.

Little children dashed by out of the dark like fireflies. Their crepe-paper dresses and butterfly wings were not made for running and we heard more than one rip, dryly, and the regretful 'uh uh' that followed.

The school blazed without gaiety. The windows seemed cold and unfriendly from the lower hill. A sense of ill-fated timing crept over me, and if Momma hadn't reached for my hand I would have drifted back to Bailey and Uncle Willie, and possibly beyond. She made a few slow jokes about my feet getting cold, and tugged me along to the now-strange building.

Around the front steps, assurance came back. There were my fellow 'greats', the graduating class. Hair brushed back, legs oiled, new dresses and pressed pleats, fresh pocket handkerchiefs and little handbags, all home-sewn. Oh, we were up to snuff, all right. I joined my comrades and didn't even see my family go in to find seats in the crowded auditorium.

The school band struck up a march and all classes filed in as had been rehearsed. We stood in front of our seats, as assigned, and on a signal from the choir director, we sat. No sooner had this been accomplished than the band started to play the national anthem. We rose again and sang the song, after which we recited the pledge of allegiance. We remained standing for a brief minute before the choir director and the principal signaled to us, rather desperately I thought, to take our seats. The command was so unusual that our carefully rehearsed and smooth-running machine was thrown off. For a full minute we fumbled for our chairs and bumped into each other awkwardly. Habits change or solidify under pressure, so in our state of nervous tension we had been ready to follow our usual assembly pattern: the American national anthem, then the pledge of allegiance, then the song every Black person I knew called the Negro National Anthem. All done in the same key, with the same passion and most often standing on the same foot.

Finding my seat at last, I was overcome with a presentiment of worse things to come. Something unrehearsed, unplanned, was going to happen, and we were going to be made to look bad. I distinctly remember being explicit in the choice of pronoun. It was 'we', the graduating class, the unit, that concerned me then.

The principal welcomed 'parents and friends' and asked the Baptist minister to lead us in prayer. His invocation was brief and punchy, and for a second I thought we were getting back on the high road to right action. When the principal came back to the dais, however, his voice had changed. Sounds always affected me profoundly and the principal's voice was one of my favorites. During assembly it melted and lowed weakly into the audience. It had not been in my plan to listen to him, but my curiosity was piqued and I straightened up to give him my attention.

He was talking about Booker T. Washington, our 'late great leader', who said we can be as close as the fingers on the hand, etc. . . . Then he said a few vague things about friendship and the friendship of kindly people to those less forunate than themselves. With that his voice nearly faded, thin, away. Like a river diminishing to a stream and then to a trickle. But he cleared his throat and said, 'Our speaker tonight, who is also our friend, came from Texarkana to deliver the commencement address, but due to the irregularity of the train schedule, he's going to, as they say, "speak and run".' He said that we understood and wanted the man to know that we were most grateful for the time he was able to give us and then something about how we were willing always to adjust to another's program, and without more ado – 'I give you Mr Edward Donleavy.'

Not one but two white men came through the door off-stage. The shorter one walked to the speaker's platform, and the tall one moved over to the center seat and sat down. But that was our principal's seat, and already occupied. The dislodged gentleman bounced around for a long breath or two before the Baptist minister gave him his chair, then with more dignity than the situation deserved, the minister walked off the stage.

Donleavy looked at the audience once (on reflection, I'm sure that he wanted only to reassure himself that we were really there), adjusted his glasses and began to read from a sheaf of papers.

He was glad 'to be here and to see the work going on just as it was in the other schools'.

At the first 'Amen' from the audience I willed the offender to immediate death by choking on the word. But Amen's and Yes, sir's began to fall around the room like rain through a ragged umbrella.

He told us of the wonderful changes we children in Stamps

had in store. The Central School (naturally, the white school was Central) had already been granted improvements that would be in use in the fall. A well-known artist was coming from Little Rock to teach art to them. They were going to have the newest microscopes and chemistry equipment for their laboratory. Mr Donleavy didn't leave us long in the dark over who made these improvements available to Central High. Nor were we to be ignored in the general betterment scheme he had in mind.

He said that he had pointed out to people at a very high level that one of the first-line football tacklers at Arkansas Agricultural and Mechanical College had graduated from good old Lafayette County Training School. Here fewer Amen's were heard. Those few that did break though lay dully in the air with the heaviness of habit.

He went on to praise us. He went on to say how he had bragged that 'one of the best basketball players at Fisk sank his first ball right here at Lafayette County Training School.'

The white kids were going to have a chance to become Galileos and Madame Curies and Edisons and Gauguins, and our boys (the girls weren't even in on it) would try to be Jesse Owenses and Joe Louises.

Owens and the Brown Bomber were great heroes in our world, but what school official in the white-goddom of Little Rock had the right to decide that those two men must be our only heroes? Who decided that for Henry Reed to become a scientist he had to work like George Washington Carver, as a bootblack, to buy a lousy microscope? Bailey was obviously always going to be too small to be an athlete, so which concrete angel glued to what country seat had decided that if my brother wanted to become a lawyer he had to first pay penance for his skin by picking cotton and hoeing corn and studying correspondence books at night for twenty years?

The man's dead words fell like bricks around the auditorium and too many settled in my belly. Constrained by hard-learned manners I couldn't look behind me, but to my left and right the proud graduating class of 1940 had dropped their heads. Every girl in my row had found something new to do with her handkerchief. Some folded the tiny squares into love knots, some into triangles, but most were wadding them, then pressing them flat on their yellow laps.

On the dais, the ancient tragedy was being replayed. Professor Parsons sat, a sculptor's reject, rigid. His large, heavy body seemed devoid of will or willingness, and his eyes said he was no longer with us. The other teachers examined the flag (which was draped stage right) or their notes, or the windows which opened on our now-famous playing diamond.

Graduation, the hush-hush magic time of frills and gifts and congratulations and diplomas, was finished for me before my name was called. The accomplishment was nothing. The meticulous maps, drawn in three colors of ink, learning and spelling decasyllabic words, memorizing the whole of *The Rape of Lucrece* – it was for nothing. Donleavy had exposed us.

We were maids and farmers, handymen and washerwomen, and anything higher that we aspired to was farcical and presumptuous.

Then I wished that Gabriel Prosser and Nat Turner had killed all whitefolks in their beds and that Abraham Lincoln had been assassinated before the signing of the Emancipation Proclamation, and that Harriet Tubman had been killed by that blow on her head and Christopher Columbus had drowned in the *Santa María*.

It was awful to be Negro and have no control over my life. It was brutal to be young and already trained to sit quietly and listen to charges brought against my color with no chance of defense. We should all be dead. I thought I should like to see us all dead, one on top of the other. A pyramid of flesh with the whitefolks on the bottom, as the broad base, then the Indians with their silly tomahawks and teepees and wigwams and treaties, the Negroes with their mops and recipes and cotton sacks and spirituals sticking out of their mouths. The Dutch children should all stumble in their wooden shoes and break their necks. The French should choke to death on the Louisiana Purchase (1803) while silkworms ate all the Chinese with their stupid pigtails. As a species, we were an abomination. All of us.

Donleavy was running for election, and assured our parents that if he won we could count on having the only colored paved playing field in that part of Arkansas. Also – he never looked up to acknowledge the grunts of acceptance – also, we were bound to get some new equipment for the home economics building and the workshop.

He finished, and since there was no need to give any more than the most perfunctory thank-you's, he nodded to the men on the stage, and the tall white man who was never introduced joined him at the door. They left with the attitude that now they were off to something really important. (The graduation ceremonies at Lafayette County Training School had been a mere preliminary.)

The ugliness they left was palpable. An uninvited guest who wouldn't leave. The choir was summoned and sang a modern arrangement of 'Onward, Christian Soldiers', with new words pertaining to graduates seeking their place in the world. But it didn't work. Elouise, the daughter of the Baptist minister, recited 'Invictus', and I could have cried at the impertinence of 'I am the master of my fate, I am the captain of my soul.'

My name had lost its ring of familiarity and I had to be nudged to go and receive my diploma. All my preparations had fled. I neither marched up to the stage like a conquering Amazon, nor did I look in the audience for Bailey's nod of approval. Marguerite Johnson, I heard the name again, my honors were read, there were noises in the audience of appreciation, and I took my place on the stage as rehearsed.

I thought about colors I hated: ecru, puce, lavender, beige and black.

There was shuffling and rustling around me, then Henry Reed was giving his valedictory address, 'To Be or Not to Be'.

Hadn't he heard the whitefolks? We couldn't *be*, so the question was a waste of time. Henry's voice came out clear and strong. I feared to look at him. Hadn't he got the message? There was no 'nobler in the mind' for Negroes because the world didn't think we had minds, and they let us know it. 'Outrageous fortune'? Now, that was a joke. When the ceremony was over I had to tell Henry Reed some things. That is, if I still cared. Not 'rub', Henry, 'erase'. 'Ah, there's the erase.' Us.

Henry had been a good student in elocution. His voice rose on tides of promise and fell on waves of warnings. The English teacher had helped him to create a sermon winging through Hamlet's soliloquy. To be a man, a doer, a builder, a leader, or to be a tool, an unfunny joke, a crusher of funky toadstools. I marveled that Henry could go through with the speech as if we had a choice.

I had been listening and silently rebutting each sentence with my eyes closed; then there was a hush, which in an audience warns that something unplanned is happening. I looked up and saw Henry Reed, the conservative, the proper, the A student, turn his back to the audience and turn to us (the proud graduating class of 1940) and sing, nearly speaking,

> 'Lift ev'ry voice and sing
> Till earth and heaven ring
> Ring with the harmonies of Liberty . . .'*

It was the poem written by James Weldon Johnson. It was the music composed by J. Rosamond Johnson. It was the Negro national anthem. Out of habit we were singing it.

Our mothers and fathers stood in the dark hall and joined the hymn of encouragement. A kindergarten teacher led the small children on to the stage and the buttercups and daisies and bunny rabbits marked time and tried to follow:

* 'Lift Ev'ry Voice and Sing' – words by James Weldon Johnson and music by J. Rosamond Johnson. Copyright by Edward B. Marks Music Corporation. Used by permission.

'Stony the road we trod
Bitter the chastening rod
Felt in the days when hope, unborn, had died.
Yet with a steady beat
Have not our weary feet
Come to the place for which our fathers sighed?'

Every child I knew had learned that song with his ABC's and along with 'Jesus Loves Me This I Know'. But I personally had never heard it before. Never heard the words, despite the thousands of times I had sung them. Never thought they had anything to do with me.

On the other hand, the words of Patrick Henry had made such an impression on me that I had been able to stretch myself tall and trembling and say, 'I know not what course others may take, but as for me, give me liberty or give me death.'

And now I heard, really for the first time:

'We have come over a way that with tears
has been watered,
We have come, treading our path through
the blood of the slaughtered.'

While echoes of the song shivered in the air, Henry Reed bowed his head, said 'Thank you', and returned to his place in the line. The tears that slipped down many faces were not wiped away in shame.

We were on top again. As always, again. We survived. The depths had been icy and dark, but now a bright sun spoke to our souls. I was no longer simply a member of the proud graduating class of 1940; I was a proud member of the wonderful, beautiful Negro race.

Oh, Black known and unknown poets, how often have your auctioned pains sustained us? Who will compute the lonely nights made less lonely by your songs, or the empty pots made less tragic by your tales?

If we were a people much given to revealing secrets, we might raise monuments and sacrifice to the memories of our poets, but slavery cured us of that weakness. It may be enough, however, to have it said that we survive in exact relationship to the dedication of our poets (include preachers, musicians and blues singers).

*This extract is from* I Know Why the Caged Bird Sings *(Virago, 1984)*

# SCARLETT MccGWIRE

......................................

## *I Will Go to London, I Will*

I *was born in Swanage, Dorset, in 1953. My father was in the navy until I was thirteen so we lived all over the place, including Moscow and the United States. This meant I went to lots of schools, so I became a boarder at Beaminster Comprehensive at eleven. The fourth and fifth years were pretty awful and at sixteen I was sent to Atlantic College, which is a mixed international sixth form college where we were all supposed to become world leaders – or so we understood the theory. In fact my friends and I just had a great time, with the consequent suffering of exam results. I went to Canada for a year to get out of education, then came back and read psychology at Exeter University, which did not do a lot for me.*

*I was thirteen when I decided to be a journalist, after realising I had neither the looks nor the talent to be an actress. I get bored easily, so I have not had a career as such but have just done lots of things which interest me – worked on newspapers, been a radio and television reporter. I now do mainly television and features for the* Guardian *and the* Observer.

*I wrote a book – Kim's Story – about a former boyfriend who was in a motorbike accident and suffered brain damage which caused amnesia. I live in north London with my son Pascoe, Christian and, half the week, his daughter Molly.*

......................................

It was two days before the Easter holidays when Myra told me David wanted to go out with me.

I did not really believe it. At first I assumed she was messing around, then wondered if it was a cruel joke by some people who thought I had a rather inflated idea of myself. After all, what would David be doing looking at me?

His last two girlfriends had both been boarders, so I knew them well. They were exceptionally good-looking, witty and in the years above me. They had a maturity which entirely eluded me.

I was just a desperately ordinary fourteen-year-old third year. He could hardly be impressed by my looks – nor could it be my brains, since he had barely spoken to me. I could remember once in the last few weeks he had joked with me as we passed in a corridor, but that could hardly be the seed of a grand passion.

By the time my mother arrived to take me and my two sisters back to the depths of mid-Wales for the holdiays, nothing had been heard directly from him although Myra still stuck to her story that she had been a genuine messenger. With a slight feeling of disappointment, I put it out of my mind.

We lived twelve miles outside Aberystwyth in a dilapidated farmhouse at the end of a mile of unmade-up track. The house had been built on a bog and the damp seeped through so freely that a mushroom was growing on the wall in my parents' bedroom when we moved in the previous September. My father had decided to leave the navy and take a degree at Aberystwyth University, so this was only our second school holiday there and we knew almost no one our own age.

Days were spent reading books and evenings watching television, with the only excitement provided by going into Aberystwyth to shop or watch a film at the local fleapit, which had the limited choice of a town isolated from the rest of civilisation.

When David's letter arrived I was first merely grateful for a break in the tedious monotony, but then grew overwhelmed by his formal request to go out with me. There was never a doubt that the answer would be anything but yes. Of course I no more knew him than he knew me, but that was different. I may just have been an anonymous third year, but he was special. After all, he had gone out with Rosa and Jackie, and broken both their hearts. I was still bemused as to why he had picked on me.

He sent me Black Magic chocolates for an Easter present,

which delighted me, although I liked neither dark chocolate nor filled sweets. I preferred Easter eggs, but when he told me he could not count how many pieces the chocolate egg I had sent him by return had arrived in, I realised his practical streak was more effective than my romanticism.

When my mother drove us back to Dorset for school, I persuaded her to drop me off where David had arranged to meet me, so we had some time together before I was subjected to the strict timetabling of boarding-house life. We leaned against a gate, talked and kissed, and I fell in love.

It did not have very much to do with him; stopping me would have taken some deliberate effort on his part: he would have had to be purposely obnoxious. Nurtured on a diet of romantic novels, teenage magazines and pop songs, my heart had been waiting for a conqueror. And suddenly David appeared: tall, blond, large blue eyes, charming and adoring. My ideal might have been dark with brown eyes, but Paul McCartney and all the other idols were just fantasies: this was a real person to love. I can remember not a word of what we talked about that afternoon or any other time. There is no enduring wit, nor wisdom. Yet from that afternoon on every available moment was spent with him and I always wanted more of his company.

Time was rationed to the school break and lunch hour (which we used fully by not eating lunch) and the hour after school. This was very much stolen time, as the girl boarders were allowed to stay after school only if they were doing an approved and supervised activity. At breakfast a book was sent round to sign if we were going to be late back and daily I would diligently sign, putting down any activity which came to mind.

Missing lunch was no imposition, because I could have eaten nothing anyway. Love had taken me over completely, entirely filling my stomach, so that I only picked at my breakfast bowl of cornflakes. I laughed at the memory of my previous attempts at diets, which always failed in the competition with my ravenous appetite and the temptation of tantalising food on offer. I had found the key to the perfect diet and would now float painlessly down to the precious goal of eight stone.

I allowed myself to be totally consumed by Love. Lessons were spent waiting to see David. Back at the boarding house, prep was two hours of daydreaming. Time without David was just minutes and hours to be frittered away until we were together again.

I still had no idea what David had ever seen in me, but decided it could have had nothing to do with the real me, so I desperately tried to keep up an image I hoped he would continue to like. I had a rather striking, but desperately unfashionable umbrella with large turquoise flowers on it. When it rained I would walk to school with it, but I would persuade Christine to carry it back while I was accompanied by David so that he never saw it.

When Christine was mocking me and telling people how silly I was, Rosa sympathised, saying that when she went out with David, she would never let him even see her blowing her nose. The very next Saturday I spent the whole morning with David with a blocked nose, refusing to use a hankie to relieve it. I sniffed and snorted my way through the day, which must have been far more offensive than innocently blowing my nose.

David could have demanded anything from me. My virginity, which I would fight so hard to keep over the next few years, would have been willingly given if I had only been aware of its importance and how much he must have wanted it. He found my innocence impenetrable. One day after school we had taken shelter from the rain in some garages, which gave us some unaccustomed privacy, and he started undoing my bra. When I giggled and told him to stop, he explained he was just seeing if he could do it. So when he had snapped it open I simply told him to do it up again, believing he was interested only in his mechanical skill. He tried but found it impossible; while he had probably become quite practised at undoing them, I doubt if he had ever been asked to do one up before.

It was those sessions after school which were to be our undoing. I was not devious enough to go straight back occasionally to the boarding house to calm the suspicions of the house mistress. Even when I felt the net was closing in, I did not stop for a few days in the hope of resuming later.

One day when we were again sheltering in the garages the housemistress, Mrs Cox, came out to find me. Her look of shocked revulsion when she saw us shamed me. Her dirty mind succeeded in smearing what we were doing.

I was marched straight back to the boarding house, lectured as to my morality and told I was to be up before the headmaster in the morning.

The headmaster was the sort of man who spent Divinity lessons either talking about sex or berating the Labour government because its only achievement, in his eyes, had been to legalise homosexuality, which went against God's teachings. This was the first time I had been sent to him for punishment. He was not as unpleasant as Mrs Cox, but the effect was worse. He not only pronounced my punishment of being gated – confined to the boarding house when not in school – for two weeks, but made it quite clear that my behaviour was to be exemplary during that time, which specifically included seeing a lot less of David.

At first, David was extremely sympathetic. He was a day boy, not subject to the awful discipline of a boarding house, but he understood that life was rather unpleasant for me. However, when he discovered I was scared of being seen with him, in case anyone should think I was deliberately flouting the headmaster, he found the impositions of the boarding house tiring. He suggested we did not see each other until the punishment was over. While I minded the decision, a part of me was relieved; I was beginning to feel torn between the demands of David and the wrath of the authorities.

The day my punishment ended there was a ten-mile sponsored walk for Oxfam. Even the girl boarders were to be allowed to spend the whole day walking instead of the two hours of free time allowed on a Saturday morning, because it was for charity. It seemed a suitable celebration.

The night before the walk Myra came with another message from David: he did not want to go out with me again.

I managed a mechanical smile and muttered that I understood, before turning away. The gong for tea sounded and I had to behave as normal, while the clatter of cutlery upon crockery and the surrounding conversations all seemed distant. Even lifting the fork to my mouth was an effort, as my appetite had been completely subsumed by nausea since Myra's message. My limbs felt heavy and my head ached so much it felt as if it were encased in a tightening metal band.

In bed that night I tried to do a deal with God, promising Him anything if the message was wrong, and threatening not to believe if David truly did not want to see me again.

Part of me did not believe the message. After all, Myra was far from being a close friend of David's, as he did not even like her. And what had changed between us?

When I woke the next day to the sunshine of a cloudless sky, I hoped it was an omen: perfect weather for our reunion. However, a night of little sleep and vivid dreams had only worsened my headache and my general feeling of heaviness, reminding me how unpleasant the day might be.

As soon as I saw him in the town square, I knew it was over: he slunk away, unable to face me. He had told Myra to avoid having to tell me. The last hope extinguished, I felt leaden.

Somehow I walked those ten miles, picking up one heavy foot to put it in front of the other. I had started in the same large group as David, but lagged further and further behind as he strode ahead.

That weekend was only made bleaker by the perpetual sunshine. Monday was to be worse. My best friend Cherry told me David had asked her to go out with him. The decision was mine – if I minded a lot, she would not do it. I knew refusing would not get David back, so I told her she could do as she pleased. In truth I wished she would turn him down without me having to ask. She never realised just how much I cared.

For the next few weeks it was Cherry who left our group every break and every lunchtime. I always knew where they were and would enviously watch them from a distance. As Cherry was a day girl, they did not have the restrictions which I had suffered. David and I were not to talk again for a year.

I could never work out whether it was infuriating or reassuring that Cherry was never smitten like me. For her David was only bait, to show someone else that other boys found her attractive. She would come back to us and moan about him. While I would have done anything to be in her position, she was contemptuous of it and of him.

As I had told her I did not mind – and she was the only person I could possible have confided in – there was nobody I could talk to about it. I had an automatic smile for use in company and could laugh as heartily as the rest, while inside I felt I was being gnawed away. Each day was to be endured.

In those summer evenings I would quite often walk alone in the garden of the boarding house. Even now the sound of evening birdsong in the early summer brings on a sharp sadness.

All the beautiful music of summer 1968 which had made me bubble over in the early days of that term merely made me more aware of my loss. I lived through every emotional cliché of every song about losing in love. I remember Bobby Kennedy, who was going for the Democratic nomination for the American presidency, being shot one Wednesday. Some boy who went home for lunch brought the news back on his return and through the afternoon, as I sat in needlework making a dress I had wanted to wear with David – empire line, with a white lacy bodice and blue skirt – we had updated bulletins. By the end of the school day he had died. While everyone else went round wailing – in retrospect a surprising reaction from teenagers in an isolated rural school to an event on the other side of the world – I just wished for something that obvious to grieve over; something which would affect me.

I was already fascinated by news and watched the student revolt of '68 unfold on television. This only made the feeling that everything was passing me by worse – I was watching world events outside, while trapped inside, desperately wanting to be part of a bigger world where I could forget David.

We had a wonderful English teacher, Dave Lambert, who was more interested in capturing our attention than in syntax and grammar. He introduced us to modern literature and would sometimes show films. They were always good enough to overcome the primitive equipment – the sound track was accompanied by the hum of the projector and the images appeared on a creased screen, while we sat on rows of canvas chairs in the school assembly hall.

On one of those miserable days I filed in to watch *Billy Liar*, which I hoped would while away the morning. In black and white, it told the story of Billy, who lives in a provincial town working at an undertaker's and manages to make his painfully mundane life passable only by drifting into fantasies about the country of his dreams, Ambrosia. There, he is leader, adored by the populace and always performing heroic deeds. His fantasies are not entirely restricted to Ambrosia and his rather ambivalent relationship with the truth means he is forever in trouble in real life. Billy does have a talent for words, writing songs and comic scripts. He sees this as his possible escape route, his passage to fame and fortune, when his real life would be as fulfilling as any fantasy.

Back into his life comes Julie Christie, playing a woman whose name I could never remember because to me that was always what Julie Christie was like; she was so compelling I could not believe that it could be merely acting. She is one of Billy's former girlfriends who had escaped to London and was back on a day trip.

This was the day Billy's lies were beginning to catch up with him. Both young women he was engaged to began to suspect he was not playing straight; the owner of the undertaker's was asking uncomfortable questions about the calendars Billy had not posted last Christmas; his mother discovered the calendars in his closet as well as a letter to a record request show, 'Housewives' Choice', which he had never posted.

Julie suggested returning to London with her, both as a means of escape and as a way of making his contacts for the comedy scripts. He agreed, realising that if he was ever going to enjoy more than a fantasy life, this was his chance. They arranged to meet for the last train to London. He bought his ticket and got in the carriage with her. Then, just as the guard was closing the doors, he got out to buy some milk and watched the train leave with Julie Christie still on board. He had bottled out.

I was stunned. It seemed a message for all those like me stuck in the backwaters of provincial England: go for it. There was a simple choice: one could either wallow in dreams and stay stuck in a rut or get up one's courage and go.

When the curtains were drawn to let in the light I turned to my friends, wanting to talk about it. We might have been watching different films: they talked about how funny it was. For them there was no allegory.

It was as if for the first time I had been spoken to in a language I could understand. The fact that few other people had heard it made it more pertinent. Instead of feeling inadequate and desperately trying to change myself because I never truly seemed to fit in, now I could accept that I did not fit because I was different. I knew that I would leave; my life would not pan out in Dorset on the terms of the teachers and pupils of Beaminster School, where any aspirations or ambitions were stamped upon.

I would also leave David behind and have raging affairs with exciting men. I was suffering only temporary pain, whatever agony it was putting me through. This perspective did not stop me wanting David: I was to learn over and over that there is nothing rational about love or passion. Knowing it was not going to last, and that there was an exciting future without him, was the beginning of recovery.

It was to be another ten years before I made it to London – another school, university, and even a first job in the West Country intervened. Through those years it was Billy and Julie who kept me going. I was not going to be stuck living out a fantasy because life was too awful.

I remember over and over, when I felt beaten, gritting my teeth and saying: 'I will be Julie Christie, I will go to London.'

# JANINA BAUMAN

## *Love in the Warsaw Ghetto*

I *was born in Warsaw in 1926. My father, grandfather and most of my uncles were doctors. Although I was Jewish, I was brought up in Polish rather than Jewish tradition.*

*I was just thirteen when the Second World War began. My father went to fight the Nazis and never came back. With my mother and younger sister I was forced to move into the Jewish ghetto and live there in appalling conditions for over two years. Hiding in some awful places, we survived mass deportations to the death camps and later escaped beyond the ghetto walls to spend two more years running away and hiding.*

*After the war I completed my school education and took my BA in social sciences and my MA in aesthetics at the University of Warsaw. I married, had three daughters and for twenty years worked in Polish Film, mainly as a script editor.*

*In 1968 my family had to leave Poland for political reasons. After three years in Israel, we settled in Leeds. Here, having learnt English almost from scratch and after a crash course in librarianship at Leeds Polytechnic, I was appointed assistant librarian in a big comprehensive school, where I worked for five years until an early retirement. Only then did I take to writing. I* have written two autobiographical books: Winter in the Morning, A Young Girl's Life in the Warsaw Ghetto and Beyond *and* A Dream of Belonging, My Years in Postwar Poland. 'Love in the Warsaw Ghetto' *is based on* Winter in the Morning.

*All my life writing was my favourite occupation but only now I have become a full-time writer. At the moment I am trying to write a novel.*

My granddaughter Sophie is fifteen. Not quite yet, she will be in three months' time but prefers to say she's fifteen now. Next year she'll be taking her O levels. She hardly ever finds time to pay me a visit. But I don't blame her: why should she sit and talk to an old woman when she has so many things to do and such a lot of friends to be with? Besides, she finds my English funny and because of it, I guess, she sees me as a stranger. Or rather as someone not as familiar and taken for granted as her other Gran, who – like herself – is from Yorkshire, and always treats her to her delicious scones and crumpets. I can't offer her anything like that. I'm a lousy cook and have never baked a thing in my whole life. I'm much better at telling stories. But Sophie doesn't seem much interested in my stories. Except for last night.

Yesterday my daughter Silvia phoned to say that Sophie was in bed with tonsillitis, and – poor girl – would be on her own all day long. So could you, Mama, please come over and keep her company? Of course I could and, turning a deaf ear to my good old man's grumbling, went to sit with Sophie.

It was the first time, I think, we had spent so many hours together, just the two of us. Despite her sore throat, Sophie talked a lot and even listened to what I had to say, interrupting only from time to time to correct my pronunciation:

'It's *road*, Grannie, *road* and not *rod*. You keep clipping your *o*'s. And when you say *bread* it always sounds like *bret*. Why on earth can't you learn to speak properly?'

'Because I was born and brought up in Poland and my language is Polish. You know that. All Poles speak English like me. It's not our fault. You should feel happy that you were born in this country, can stay here all your life if only you wish, and don't have to worry about how you speak, not to mention all sorts of other, more important matters. You are a lucky girl, Sophie.' She gave me an apologetic look but did not say she was sorry. Instead she began to explain that she, too, had her own doubts and worries.

'I don't know why Mum and Dad and you, Grannie, imagine that I'm happy day and night. I'm not. And no one ever asks me why.'

I asked. As if she could hardly wait to start talking, Sophie told me what troubled her straight away. She longed to have a boyfriend. Her best friend Sue had been going out with a boy since last summer. Every girl in her class seemed to have someone. They all knew about kissing and things like that, while she, Sophie, had only to pretend she knew because, in fact, she had never kissed a boy and always refused if a boy tried to kiss her.

'I feel so old, Grannie, and so stupid . . .'

Suddenly, her words struck a familiar chord. I knew what she felt. I used to feel the same when I was her age, an old maid of fifteen. Is it possible that it was such a long time ago, forty-five years or even more? I felt it all afresh and smiled at my thoughts.

'You see, Grannie, you smile!'

'I smile at my memories. Would you like to hear a story?'

'What story?'

'The story of my first love.'

'But it must have been ages ago! You can't possibly remember.'

'Oh yes, I do. One doesn't forget such moments. They stay with you for ever. With full particulars. It happened during the third year of the war . . .'

'War! Oh no! I've got enough of it at school. Just finished writing an essay about Hitler.'

'It isn't going to be about Hitler but about me, a girl with dark hair and green eyes like yours, who was fifteen years and six months old when it all began. At first it has to have something to do with Hitler, after all, although I've promised not to mention him. You must have heard how he hated the Jews, and what he did to them.'

'I know, I know . . . The concentration camps . . . the gas

chambers . . . six million people murdered by the Nazis . . . Save your breath, Grannie.'

'You also know that I'm Jewish and lived in Warsaw then, under the German occupation. And so I was one of those they intended to murder.'

'Honestly, it has never crossed my mind.'

'All right. You know it now. Half a million Jews were locked in the Warsaw ghetto behind high walls topped with barbed wire. The gates of the ghetto were heavily guarded by German, Polish and Jewish police. There were not enough houses to shelter all. The flats were overcrowded and there were thousands and thousands of homeless. They lived in the streets begging for food and died on the pavements from starvation and infectious diseases, mainly from typhus. On the other hand, people like my family, who had some money and precious things left from before the war, and a roof over their heads, no matter how small, tried hard to make something of their lives in these inhuman conditions. My mother, my younger sister Sophie and I were lucky because we found somewhere to live in the ghetto. It was a tiny little flat on the top floor of a six-storey apartment house. The three of us lived in a small room, my aunt and uncle in the second one, and my aunt's father in the corridor, between the kitchen and the loo. There was no bathroom in the flat. Yet we were extremely lucky to have this flat for ourselves, with no need to share it with strangers. We didn't starve either, at least not at the beginning, because we could afford to buy food from the black market that, against all odds, thrived in the ghetto at the time. It was not particularly good food and I never had enough to eat, but it was not starving.'

'What did you do? Did you go to school?'

'No. There were no schools in the ghetto. But there were many teachers and a lot of children who wanted to learn. So they studied in small groups, at home. And so did I, with seven other girls. We met every day in someone's flat and a teacher joined us. One day it was maths, next day science, or Polish, or history, and so on. If we were discovered by the Nazis they would have shot us dead because studying was forbidden, not only in the ghetto but everywhere under the German occupation. But at the beginning the Nazis rarely entered the ghetto: they feared they might catch lice and typhus from us.

'Day after day, on my way to the lessons and back, I walked along the streets strewn with dying people and corpses covered with newspapers held down with bricks. I could hardly put up with it. I was terribly sorry for those people and felt guilty about being well fed when they were starving. I often gave my bread or a little money to the begging children, but it couldn't save them. My friends felt the same way and we kept wondering what could we do to help. At last we found something to do.'

'But Grannie, you promised to tell me about your first love . . .'

'Be patient, my dear, it's coming up. But not just yet. First I must tell you about my work in the ghetto. My friends and I soon came across some people who found a way of helping the destitute by growing vegetables for them on every free bit of ground they could find within the ghetto walls. It needed volunteers who would work without being paid. All eight of us joined the organisation and were sent to grow carrots, beetroots and tomatoes in our spare time. We worked on the grounds of a ruined hospital and had to clear them from debris before we could start gardening. You may find it hard to believe, but I enjoyed this work enormously. It was quiet there, we were cut off from the appalling streets by green trees and shrubs. So, during my working hours I could forget about the hell I lived in. Boys and girls worked together. We had a very handsome young instructor called Tadek . . .'

'And you fell in love with him . . .'

'No, I didn't, although I found him very attractive. My friend Rena did, and he fell in love with her. Rena was fifteen, like myself, and not particularly pretty: she was skinny and her face was a bit flat. But she was a very gentle girl, sensitive and thoughtful, and Tadek clearly lost his head over her. He chose her to be his assistant and together they looked after an incubator that was offered to our group to start a chicken farm. They were always together, tending the hatching eggs, feeding the chickens, and spending every moment of their spare time with each other. Rena seemed very happy. She changed a lot. Stopped chatting with us. Walked as if in a dream. Her eyes became hazy, all her behaviour vague.

'I envied her terribly. Not because I fancied Tadek, which I didn't, but because she was in love and someone was in love with her. The other girls in my group flirted with the boys and there was a lot of kissing going on in the bushes. But it was not the same. I didn't envy them. I could have done it, too, if only I'd wanted. Another good friend of mine, Zula, felt exactly like myself. We often talked about Rena and wondered why it was happening to her and not to us. We were both far more attractive then Rena, particularly Zula, who had fiery red hair, a milky complexion faintly dotted with freckles, and lively eyes that reminded me of shiny little cherries. We came to the conclusion that beauty had little to do with love and felt miserable, lonely, and unwanted because we loved nobody and nobody was in love with us.'

'If I were there I would have joined you and Zula,' said Sophie. 'You had each other, at least, and I'm on my own and have no one to talk to about this kind of thing since Sue got involved with Peter.'

'Poor Sophie! I know how it feels. But listen. Some time later, in the winter, my grandma, who also lived in the ghetto, took me to a café. Yes, it must sound strange to you: a café in such an awful place. But there were some, very few. You see, people could hardly bear to think about death all the time; they needed to relax, to forget for a short while about fear and misery. So they went to the café if they could afford it.

'I sat with my grandma in this shabby place, sipped a

disgusting dark liquid that was supposed to be coffee, and didn't enjoy it a bit. There was some entertainment going on, some singing and sketches, but it was rude and not at all funny. When the programme came to an end, a small band began to play and a few couples went to the dancing floor. Suddenly someone approached my grandma and very politely asked her to let him dance with me. It was a young fellow about my own age, looking very tidy and a little shy. Grandma, who was a forbidding kind of a person, eyed him up and down and with an air of total disapproval said she didn't mind. I didn't mind, either.

'So I danced a tango with a stranger, feeling thrilled and guilty at the same time, since I didn't approve of having too much fun when people were dying in the streets. I even told my partner this, but he smiled and said: "We, too, can die very soon, you and I." It was true. I smiled back, quite relieved. I liked that boy. His eyes were blue and sparkling, his hair was fair and soft. I could feel its softness because it gently skimmed my temple as we danced: he was just a little taller than myself. And just a little older. He told me it was his sixteenth birthday that day; his parents had taken him to the café to celebrate. He too was disgusted with the programme. We couldn't talk any more because the band had changed from the sluggish tango to *Rosamunda*, a very loud and fast piece of music which was very popular everywhere in Europe during the war. Here in England it went: *Roll out the barrel* . . . and so on. But the Polish words were different. *Ro-sa-munda, you came with the northern wind* . . . sang the young pianist in the café. One could not talk with *Rosamunda* in the air, one could only dance. So we danced till the band stopped. As we walked back to my table, I dearly hoped Grandma would invite my dancer to sit with us for a while. But instead she said it was time to go home. The boy bowed politely to her, waved his hand to me, and disappeared. He didn't tell me his name. And I didn't tell him mine.'

'And so it ended? Was that what you call your first love?' Sophie sounded disappointed.

'Oh no, it was only the beginning. But then I believed I'd never meet this boy again.

'Winter came to an end. I was busy studying as usual and in my spare time worked growing vegetables again. It was a horrifying time. More and more people were dying from hunger in the streets, more and more often the Nazis entered the ghetto to arrest the innocent people or shoot them dead at random. By the beginning of the summer very worrying rumours began to be heard. Nobody was sure whether it was true, but rumour had it that the Nazis wanted to clear Warsaw of Jews and send us all away, to the labour camps, where we would certainly die from exhaustion. From day to day there was less and less hope that we would survive the war. But there was nothing we could do to prevent what was coming, so we just got on with our daily concerns as before.

'Living in constant fear and with no hope for the future, some people became very keen on enjoying themselves. The girls and boys I worked with often met after work and had parties at night. Zula and I heard gossip about these parties, but neither of us was ever invited to join them. So we were both dying to know what it all was about. Zula thought we should simply go there and join the others without an invitation, but I said "No" – I never went anywhere uninvited; besides, those young people were older than we were and not our close friends. So, one night, Zula went to a party on her own, not even telling me about her intention in advance. Next morning, when we met at work, she looked miserable. She could hardly wait to tell me what had happened to her last night. The party took place in the flat of a girl called Joanna. Twelve people were there, six boys and six girls, all almost eighteen. Zula was the thirteenth and the youngest, but Joanna and her friends didn't mind having her with them. They were playing a game when she came in. It involved sitting on each other's knees and kissing. From time to time they would drink vodka straight from the bottle. Somebody passed Zula the bottle and she drank, too.

When the bottle was empty one of the boys got another and they sent it round again. After a while Zula felt tipsy, but she could remember they danced, then switched the light off and lay down on the carpet, all next to each other. She fell asleep straight away, but woke up after a time and heard some strange noises. She guessed a couple, or maybe two, were making love in the dark and felt so terribly uneasy that she began to sob. A boy came over to comfort her and wanted to make love to her. She hardly knew him and was very frightened, so she refused. The boy didn't seem offended, though. Very gently, as if he was an old man, he told Zula that with life being what it was in the ghetto she shouldn't wait for her one true love before making love, because she might never live that long. Zula was not sure whether he was right or wrong and wanted to hear what I thought. So we talked about it all day long. At last she came to the conclusion that the boy was right and that we'd been wasting the last bits of our lives not even trying to find out what love was. But I told her that the very idea of kissing and petting with someone I didn't love, and doing it drunk and in the presence of other people, made me totally sick. I'd rather die not knowing about love, I told her. Zula changed her mind at once and said I was right.'

'Yes, you were right, Grannie. I would feel sick, too . . . But what about that boy from the café?'

'As I said, it was at the beginning of summer 1942. In the middle of June my friends and I sat our final exams – like O levels in this country – supervised only by our own teachers, because, as I've already explained to you, all our studies were secret. Then we got a message from a group of boys who studied with the same teachers and were now sitting their finals, just as we were. They wanted to meet us and suggested throwing a dancing party when the exams were over. We were all dying to meet those boys and my friends said at once they wanted to have the party. Only Rena was not interested – she wouldn't part with Tadek even for a single evening. As for me, I had some doubts. I thought that throwing a party at a time like that was shameful. On the other hand, I longed to meet the boys, to dance, to laugh.

'In the afternoon of that day, when I was at home thinking what to do and had almost decided not to go to the party next week, suddenly two young men turned up grinning on my doorstep. To my great surprise, one of them was the stranger I'd danced with in the café three months earlier. No less surprised than myself, this time he introduced himself to me. His name was Roman. He and his friend Mark had heard I had a gramophone and came to ask me to lend it for the party. It was going to take place in Roman's flat. I was so excited and confused that I said "Yes, of course," forgetting all my doubts. For a while we stood awkwardly in the corridor discussing the details of the coming event, then talking about everything and nothing. I noticed Roman was a bright, witty fellow, not nearly as shy as I'd thought when I'd first met him. He was suntanned, his open-necked blue shirt matched his sparkling eyes, and he looked far more handsome now than he had in the winter. I was suntanned too, and knew that my light green blouse matched my eyes as well. I could see that Roman and Mark had both noticed this, and it was a nice feeling. Before they left, Roman said he would pop in just before the party to collect the gramophone and take me with him, too, which would spare me looking for the venue.

'The following days and nights were all dreams and sweet expectations. I was longing to see him again. On the appointed day, though, not Roman but Mark turned up to take me and the gramophone to the party. Roman was too busy sorting things out, he said. I tried hard not to show my disappointment.

'The party was not a success, either. The room Roman shared with his parents was large enough, but it was the only one they had, so the parents stayed there all the time. My friends giggled and behaved like silly geese, the boys talked mainly to each other, and Roman was busy with the records most of the afternoon. It all was far less exciting than I'd hoped. I danced with Roman only once and didn't enjoy it. Not very much, anyway. Then we ate some tiny little sandwiches washed down with artificial lemonade, and the party was over. When all the people had left, I stayed behind to help Roman and his parents with the tidying up. Then Roman came to help me carry the gramophone home.

'For the first time the two of us were alone in the street, except for the noisy, swarming crowd. We walked, talked and laughed all the way, finding there were lots of things to tell each other. We stopped at the entrance to my house. Roman pressed my hand and asked whether I'd like to meet him again. His bright eyes were serious this time.

'On the following evening I heard him whistling *Rosamunda* in the street below my open window. I ran down and we went for a walk again. For the next three weeks we spent all our spare time together, day after day. I was working full-time then; Roman, too, had his own duties: he earned some money giving maths lessons. So there were only the evenings left. Usually we walked in the streets, since there were no nice places to go to. Sometimes Roman would come upstairs and stay in my room till almost curfew time. My mother and my sister Sophie were always with us because there was nowhere they could go to. They both liked Roman very much. He had a special gift for telling stories and was extremely witty. We all believed he'd later become a writer or actor or both.

'It was easy to talk to Roman, it was easy to be with him. We liked the same things, read the same books. It was also good being quiet together. I wanted to be alone with him and longed for him at night, when I imagined something awful might happen to him – so many people were daily shot dead in the ghetto without any reason.

'Roman, too, longed to be alone with me. But there was nowhere to go, there was no way to be alone. The streets moaned and yelled with a thousand plaintive voices, they reeked of rotten fish and dying bodies. Wherever we turned, whatever we looked at, all was sad and ugly. So we'd run away and hide from it all in my flat. There at least we were safe from sounds and smells. But not from other people.

'One afternoon we spent sitting on the couch in the corridor. For a while there was no one around and Roman stroked my cheek, and I stroked his, and we moved close to each other. But then my aunt suddenly opened the door of her room and crossed the corridor twice, on her way to the loo and back. Then Sophie went up and down. Then my aunt's father came home from town and, winking at us, shut himself in the kitchen to let us feel undisturbed . . . It was awful . . . we so much wanted to kiss, and couldn't.'

'Why?'

'Because, you see, when I was young people wouldn't kiss in front of others. It was then something very private we wouldn't like anyone to know about. So I could hardly bear it, and asked Roman to go. My eyes filled with tears as I said it.

'As we were saying goodbye, Roman whispered something strange in my ear. He said the only way we could be left alone was to go to a hotel. There was a secret hotel in the ghetto, he said, and he had enough money to book a room for a single night. We could go there tomorrow if only I said yes. He didn't look at me as he talked about it and immediately ran away in a hurry.

'That night I couldn't get to sleep. Everybody in the flat was sound asleep, but I wouldn't have talked about it anyway. Not even to my mother. From some books I'd read and from what I'd heard from the grown-ups I knew that spending a night with a boy was a wrong, shameful thing to do if you were not married. But going to a hotel was the only way to be on our own. Yes, I wanted it, I longed to spend a whole night with Roman, to hug and kiss him, to sleep in the same bed. I loved him so much. Yes, I was sure we would go to the hotel tomorrow . . .'

'Did you go?'

'No. I didn't see Roman that day, or the day after or ever again, until the war ended. Because, you see, on that day the Nazis began the mass deportation of the ghetto people to the death camps. During the three years that followed I lived on the run and in hiding and had no idea what happened to Roman. I thought he was dead.'

'But he survived?'

'Yes, he did, and we met after the war. But it was not the same. He grew up and changed almost beyond recognition. And so did I. Our love was gone. We kept in touch for some time, and then he disappeared from my sight.'

'It was a sad story. I feel sorry for you, Grannie.'

'Oh no, Sophie! You mustn't pity me. I've kept something beautiful to remember and it's good to have such memories.'

'Do you think it could ever happen to me?' she whispered when I was kissing her goodbye.

'I very much hope so, Sophie. And when it comes, you'll have no doubt it's the real thing.'

# NELL McCAFFERTY

## *Derry's Blue Suede Shoes*

I was born in the front bedroom of my parents' home at 8 Beechwood Street, Derry City, Northern Ireland, on 28 March 1944. My home town has two names, both of them legal, only one of them acceptable to people in power. Derry is the term used by people without power, who can usually be classified as Catholic or nationalist. Londonderry is the term used by those who have power, such as the police, employers, Protestants or the British government. The prefix London is important to them – it shows who is in control.

My life cannot be summed up simply by judging the name I use for my home town. My granny, for instance, was a Protestant and my grandfather was a policeman in Derry. As I write this, I am banned from live broadcasts about Northern politics, and the same ban can now apply under the censorship rules operating in Britain, though I am not a Catholic, or a member of the IRA, or a member of Sinn Fein. Who cares? Elvis Presley was once banned from moving his hips on television. Those who really want to know what's going on in my country can always learn to lip-read.

Long before Kris Kristofferson wrote the words, I knew what the feeling was like:

> And there's nothing short of dying,
> Half as lonesome as the sound,
> Of a sleeping city sidewalk,
> Sunday morning coming down.

I grew up in Northern Ireland. It was then, and still is, a colony under the control and ownership of Great Britain. In my teenage years it was directly administered by a local parliament, known as Stormont. The majority party in Stormont was Unionist, and the religious ethic favoured by unionism was a particularly conservative form of Protestantism. This meant that the Northern Sabbath was puritan in the extreme. On Sunday everything was closed to everybody, regardless of age, class, creed or religion. The children's playgrounds were shut, cinemas locked their doors, no pubs opened, restaurants remained firmly shuttered. There were no sports fixtures.

I entered my first teenage year in 1957. Thanks to Radio Luxembourg, I knew that all over the Western world, thirteen-year-olds woke up on Sunday mornings to the call of the wild, known as rock and roll. In America, particularly, I knew that they went to the drugstore to move and groove, then on to the movies, then on to the local hop, as discos then were called. If they had done their homework all week, they were rewarded with freedom on the seventh day. God blessed America on Sundays, and told the Yanks to enjoy themselves.

My home town of Derry was poignantly different. We woke up to the sound of competing church bells, calling Catholics and Protestants to their respective services. After that, the Catholics sat around twiddling their thumbs. The Protestants continued going to church, all day, to Bible service, Sunday school, evensong. The fundamentalists had at least the consolation of hell and brimstone soul-singing in their tents.

For young people there was an empty day ahead, counting the hours until night should fall and Radio Luxembourg would come crackling over the air waves. Since youth will not sit at home, we stretched our legs in the local cemetery. It was the only place open on Sundays. It was, fortunately, a rather beautiful cemetery, situated high on the hill, with sweeping views over the town, the mountains beyond, and the sea beyond that. You couldn't actually see the sea, but you knew it was out there, and that the next landfall was New York; assuming you turned your back on England to the east.

We turned our backs to England, looked westward, and crooned the Yankee hits of the day, such as 'Blueberry Hill' by Fats Domino. This was a particularly resonant choice, since Fats sang of the wind in the willow tree, and our cemetery had a weeping willow right on the crest of the hill.

Little did we know it at the time, but one of the most famous cemeteries in the world would one day become a mecca for moody youths who want to sing the blues. The Père Lachaise in Paris today attracts all manner of teenage rebels, come to pay homage at the tomb of Jim Morrison, a member of The Doors band. They spend their sundays singing his hits over his dead body. In Derry, though, in 1957, there were no dead rock and rollers. They were all alive and elsewhere, and we were all alone: condemned, as we saw it, to a living teenage death.

Our feeling of isolation was compounded by the political situation in which we found ourselves. The Unionists had a permanent political majority in Northern Ireland. There were one million of them, and only half a million of us. We faced a future of growing old, Sunday morning coming down to the mournful sound of bells.

We knew that barely four miles away, in the Republic of Ireland, Sundays were different. Teenagers there could dance on the Sabbath and go to the cinema and play football. Because of the division of Ireland, however, they seemed like foreign people to us. We had a different system of education, different government, different money, and even vastly different accents. The Republic, in effect, was a foreign country then. We knew more about America, thanks to the movies. Youth would not stay at home, but youth did not go to foreign countries in the fifties. A bus journey to the Republic was as alien a notion then as jet travel to the Costa del Sol.

To be thirteen in Derry, in 1957, was to be repressed indeed. The Catholic Church did try to alleviate the unremitting Sabbath gloom by providing entertainment in local parish halls. This

was no help at all, given the Church's attitude to what consti-
tuted entertainment. Any form of dancing other than Ceilidh
dancing, which is the Irish equivalent of the Highland fling, was
considered satanic. That is to say, sexual. Two people moving
rhythmically together was an open temptation to commit sin, in
the eyes of the Church. It all depends on how one defines sin,
of course, but since the Catholic Church was the sole arbiter for
its faithful of what constitutes sin, there was little room for
manoeuvre. From the Church's point of view, the more space
between a dancing couple, the better. Looked at clinically, the
Church was not entirely wrong. Take, for example, the words
of a hit song of the time, which the Church banned:

> Put another nickel in,
> In that nickelodeon,
> All I want is loving you
> And music, music, music.
> I'd do anything for you,
> Anything you want me to,
> All I want is loving you
> And music, music, music.
> CLOSER, MY DEAR COME CLOSER,
> The nicest part of any melody
> Is when you're dancing close to me.
>
> So put another nickel in
> In that nickelodeon . . .

The meaning of that song is clear.

Of course we liked to get close. That did not mean we wanted
sexual intercourse. We were only thirteen, or nineteen, or
twenty-two. However, life does sometimes go wrong, and the
Church was determined that nothing would or could go wrong
while it was in charge. This made for very dull parish hall
entertainment.

The movies put on by the Church on Sunday night were no

help either. The standard non-sinful Christian fare of cowboys and Indians killing each other, and American marines combining with British tommies to wipe out the Hun, were so much old hat, we knew. We had already seen the future on the commercial cinema screens during the most exciting week of the entire decade of the fifties, and that was the week when *Rock Around the Clock* was shown in the City picture house. Rock and roll was here to stay; we knew this because we had seen it with our own eyes, sitting electrified before the screen. *Rock Around the Clock*, the movie, changed all our lives. Bill Haley and the Comets, Fats Domino, the Platters – all the great names of the new age – appeared in celluloid flesh before us. It drove us, literally, wild.

Radio Luxembourg had kept us in bed, listening while our parents slept. *Rock Around the Clock* kept us on the streets. Every teenager in town queued for hours to get into the cinema. After the first showing, the audience poured exuberantly into the streets. Now we knew how to move and groove at the same time. In the age before television, the movies showed us how to dance, which we called jiving. To the uninitiated, jiving appeared to be a very strange form of dancing indeed. It consisted of young people jerking their limbs, and boys throwing girls over their shoulders, or drawing them backwards, on their backs, between their legs, all the while speaking in a strange tongue. The boy would say, 'See you later, alligator.' The girl would reply, 'In a while, crocodile.'

Clearly, the law of the jungle was operating in the streets of Derry, and the worst fears of all the Churches were confirmed. As with so much else in Northern Ireland, the police were called in to reinforce the status quo, and they tried to sweep the young people from the dancing streets. The newspapers of the time recorded that riots had broken out, and arrests were effected. Let history record that the first person arrested and convicted was a boy from my own street, called Gerard Sharkey. Naturally he immediately became a hero, a martyr for the cause of teenage rebellion and rock and roll. I was forbidden to speak to him for at least a fortnight.

The boy who was convicted of dancing in a public thoroughfare, thereby causing a breach of the peace, did not, as confidently predicted at the time, come to a bad end. He is today the settled married father of a family, one of the few people in the United Kingdom of Great Britain and Northern Ireland actually to have a steady job.

Riots and rebellion notwithstanding, the nature of the Northern Sabbath remained unchanged. Sunday afternoon still found us disconsolate, grouped among the tombstones, howling at an imaginary moon. We were, by now, frantic, because the movies had revealed to us the new Messiah. His name was Elvis Presley. As every school child knows today, he was and is and always will be the King of Rock and Roll. I am honoured to say that it was my privilege to be on the same planet as him when he and I were growing up. I want the world to know that he, and he alone, was responsible for changing the nature of the Northern Sunday.

It so happened that at the period of which I speak, a certain kind of establishment was allowed to open for business on the Sabbath. The churches and politicians between them could find no grounds whatsoever for ordering the closure of Italian cafés on a Sunday. All a person could do in such a place was eat ice cream and drink tea. Far from being the occasion of sin, Italian cafés on Sunday were so boring that nobody ever went into them. Indeed, it would have been considered sinfully silly to waste good and scarce money buying a cup of tea round the corner, in a shop, when the same cup of tea could be had for nothing in one's own home. We only ever entered the cafés on Sunday for the purpose of buying an ice-cream cone on the way to the cemetery. So their owners sat mournfully behind the windows, just as we sat glumly around the gravesides.

Along came Elvis.

Elvis was so good that nobody wanted to spend the whole day

sitting around waiting to hear him by night on Radio Luxembourg. Elvis was so bad that Auntie Beeb wouldn't play him in broad daylight. We hungered for Elvis, yearned for Elvis, longed to be alone with Elvis. Quite simply, we adored Elvis. The Italian café owners installed jukeboxes and stocked them with Elvis records. It was as simple and revolutionary as that.

In droves we abandoned the graveyard, and in crowds we clustered into the café on a Sunday. There were no riots, no police, and no need of either. All we wanted was to be left alone with our ice cream, our tea and our King. Like angelic choirs we were, moaning and crooning and twitching in the booths. Like cherubim we were during the week, as our parents threatened us with no café on a Sunday if we didn't do as we were told. There would be no pocket money either, the ultimate sanction – the café owners insisted that we buy a little something while on their premises, and the minimum outlay was reckoned to be one cup of tea, one wafer, and one jukebox selection per customer, per hour.

Oh Elvis.

Oh Northern Sunday.

It was bliss from morning till night, to put another nickel in, in that nickelodeon, for music, music, music.

We had no television; we had no record-players; we had no cinemas; we had no dance halls in which to confront the savage fate of being refused a dance, or being refused an invitation to dance. What we did have was the independent individual dignity, girl and boy alike, of communing with the only human being on this earth who mattered. We had Elvis, all to ourselves, all day long, on the day of rest. Then the British army came along, and now we spend our Sundays back up in the cemetery mourning teenagers in their graves, but that's another story.

# EILEEN FAIRWEATHER

## *From Suicide to Survival*

*I was born in 1954 in London, educated at Catholic schools there, and read English at the University of Sussex. I am co-author, with Melanie McFadyean and Roisin McDonough, of* Only the Rivers Run Free: Northern Ireland, the Women's War *and author of* French Letters: The Life and Loves of Miss Maxine Harrison Form 4a. *I write features for many national magazines and newspapers, am currently a contributing editor of* Cosmopolitan, *and am a past winner of the* Standard/*Catherine Pakenham Award for young women journalists. I have also written stage plays and short stories for the radio and generally prefer to write in a comic vein because it stops me being maudlin. I live in Brighton and have a daughter.*

'Go for it. Don't believe a word the bastards have said about you.' When I talk with young audiences today, that is the message I want to leave with them. 'Don't let anyone else define you. You can be who you want to be.'

I see faces light up, shoulders relax, like someone's suddenly given them permission to breathe. Not all of them; there are always those who, so far, have had life handed to them on a plate, so don't understand what I am on about: struggle, pain, rebellion, transformation; how boring! What's *her* problem?

Well, you see, when I was younger I was suicidal.

That urge to self-destruct was my legacy from years as a child being mentally abused. I was sixteen when I first had my stomach pumped out, full as it was of the pills of self-hatred, accumulated over years of being got at because I was 'different': dreamy, bright, lippy; the first in my family to be educated beyond fifteen, and the cause, so my father said, of all his problems, including his lousy marriage.

So it was 'Exit Eileen' time: wipe myself out, make my excuses and leave.

Fortunately I've the constitution of an ox, and God must have had other plans for me, for against the odds I survived.

To anyone tempted to attempt suicide in order to make anyone around feel royally guilty, I'd say: Don't even think of it. Apart from anything else, it's all too easy to get the dose wrong and accidentally end up feeding yourself to the worms. To others – those who, like myself, once truly doubted whether any of it is worthwhile – I'd say: Wait. Give yourself time; with time certain pains really do pass. And, above everything else, do as I did: get yourself help; take responsibility for your life; because no one else will do that for you. And yes, I know; it's bloody scary.

It was not long after that overdose that I took myself off on the tube train to Release in London's Ladbroke Grove, a counselling service for young people with drug problems. I certainly wasn't into drugs, but it was the only vaguely 'alternative' agency I knew, having seen it written about in *Alternative London*, the early-seventies Bible for hippies, dropouts and radicals. Certainly I needed some alternative to the help that had been offered me: tranquillisers from my GP which made me more despairingly lethargic than ever; half-hour sessions once every six weeks with an uninspired trainee psychiatrist; and the ignorant love of the nuns at my convent school.

Those poor Sisters; what were they to make of me, the head girl who flipped? So sweet and well-intentioned, they packed me off from the overdose ward to their Mother House in Leamington Spa, and trotted me around their carefully tended gardens offering homilies on the healing power of nature and the consolation of Gerard Manley Hopkins's poems, while I babbled: 'But Sister, you don't know what it's like at home, my mother cuts off all her hair, I have to sleep with all the scissors in the house under my pillow.'

Mum, poor Mum, dead now, at peace at last, was into self-destruct too, as were I and my sisters; shabby, scabby creatures, we tore at our skin until it bled, pulled out our eyelashes until the rims were naked and red, and later, still hungry for punishment, scratched out the scabs. How could those sweet, caring, unmarried nuns, whose faith I so envied but could no longer share, understand the horror of a home rent by fear, mental illness and violence, when their religion forbade divorce, decreed Man to be the natural Head of Woman (yeah, Sisters, I got that message already – from his foot on my head), and persuaded women that pain was our God-decreed lot anyway? No, orthodox religion offered no solutions; I would have to look elsewhere.

By coincidence, as I sat on that tube train bound for Release in Ladbroke Grove, my father got on, too. He was going to the dog track in White City, just a few minutes away from my destination. I can't remember what lie I told him about where I was heading; I never have told him about the years I spent in therapy, trying to escape him. But I can remember it hurt, him in his best clothes cheerfully off to splash money around at the betting track, while I was off to ask strangers to rescue me in a twenty-year-old skirt of my mother's that I had chopped down in an attempt to make it the mini I couldn't afford. As my Mum always said, he had 'short arms and long pockets'; was so tight it's a surprise he didn't burst.

Release. Finally face to face with a shrink and burbling on, beating myself up verbally as I talk. Look, I'm sixteen years old and I can't sleep, but I'm not allowed sleepers because I ODed on them, I've got nine O levels but I'm going to fail my A's. I never go to school, I can't face it because I've no clothes and I'm so overweight, and worried about my mum. She's bald, she never goes out, she's tanked up on tranx and I don't know how to help her. And my dad says I should leave school anyway, all I'm fit for is a shop, maybe he's right, all I ever do is eat and eat and eat, and think about killing myself.

A long silence. Then the woman says, very gently, 'Why do you hate yourself so much? And who made you?'

I start to cry.

Was that a transforming moment? Yes, indeed. Because until then, no one had ever said: Look, it's not your fault your mum's out to lunch, and your dad's verdict of you in your suicidal bed was, 'You're not worth a bottle of cold piss.' It's not even your fault that he lays into your older sister instead of you. (Go on, Dad, why don't you hit me for a change, even if Anne is prettier than me? I can't bear the guilt of being less bruised.)

It's strange, the memories one blocks because it hurts too much to remember. I think of myself as someone who remembers everything, yet I can't at all remember the incident my mother once reminded me of, when Anne, aged fifteen, swapped Dad's violence for the lonely safety of a bedsit, her education cut short by the need to earn rent money by selling skirts. Apparently I was ironing, and when Dad turned on me, for want of Anne's blonde hair to tear, I told him he'd get the hot iron straight in his face if he so much as touched me.

That sounds like me, and sounds like him, yet until the night before our mother died I didn't even allow myself to remember precisely how physically cruel he was to Anne. Anne and I and younger sister Rosemarie – who, compared to us older two, got off lightly – were huddled on the floor outside Mum's sickroom in a human sculpture of entwined arms and tears, three grown-up daughters who might as well have been babies, so alone, save for each other. 'Why doesn't he ring?' sobbed Anne, raw and ragged after weeks of terminal nursing and, unlike me, still hoping for some protection from the man who, when she rang to say Mum was dying, sighed, 'Well, she always was a hypochondriac.'

So many memories unleashed by vodka and Coke and imminent bereavement, loss of the only parent who ever loved us, Anne for the first time in years talking of the bruises and the fractures, and me with such shame and pity remembering them too. Oh God, his big policeman's boot stomping down on her shoulder and breaking her collarbone, crunch, crunch. Daddy, why wasn't it mine?

In the hospital you told her to keep quiet, for she could lose you your job as a policeman, a protector of the community (you told me pretty much the same in my suicide bed), but silenced anger has to find some outlet. So for years my sister and I, who needed each other so much, simply hated each other, victims of your game of divide and rule, which cast me as clever but ugly, her pretty but thick; lies that weren't true of either of us.

It took my sister and me years to rediscover our old early childhood closeness. Hating each other, I suppose, at least took the edge off our self-hatred. Because for children in unhappy families, the real tragedy is that we blame ourselves for the pain in our homes. As babies, totally dependent on our parents for survival, unable to feed or even clean ourselves, we learn to associate every lapse of love with our own unloveability. Maybe that makes us feel less powerless, because then we can believe that 'If only I clean up my act, become a better child, then they'll love me.' Let's face it, the idea of serving eighteen years minimum in a home where you're always going to be dumped on, whatever you do, is pretty unpalatable. Maybe Dad's right when he says that, but for me and my snivelling sisters he and Mum would be happy, and she would have a full head of hair and enjoy being jumped on. So! Get cracking, girl! Take that Saturday job in the hairdresser's, save for the discount wig for Mum, clean your room, and generally try to minimise your existence!

Except, of course, that doesn't work. No child is to blame for adult fuck-ups. And those cowardly adults who make children carry their blame deserve to be strung up by the short and curlies. Yet that's what's happening all over Britain; there are young people who fear, because they have been made to fear, that it is their fault that Mum or Dad or both are as miserable as sin, or alcoholic, or addicted to tranx or drugs which are harder, and lash out with their fists or soul-destroying tongue or, slimily, their fingers, creeping under your bedclothes late at night because 'you provoked them'.

You didn't. You can redefine yourself. You are not necessarily who your parents, for sad, sick reasons of their own, define you as. They may need you to be their scapegoat, because they lack the strength to take responsibility for their own lives. But you don't have to remain their victim. Sure, it's difficult when you are dependent on them for the very bread in your mouth, the roof over your head, but in your heart at least you can start to set yourself free; create a small inviolate space within yourself, its colour electric blue, where you are immune to their poison and their barbs and feel no need even to respond.

Hate them, even, if that feels like the only way you can get rid of self-hatred. But beware; hatred has a funny habit of rebounding on the hater, of making an already mangled soul more twisted.

Forgiveness, understanding; how easy it is to exhort these, yet how hard I still struggle for them in terms of my father. But yes; he has his excuses too. Most people, even the most hurtful, do.

That visit to Release didn't work instant magic; I didn't turn overnight from self-destroyer into survivor. It was a long, long haul and involved many years of therapy, and more than a few wrong turnings along the way. But it was a start; acknowledging that I needed help, had a right to ask for it (neediness itself confers that right, but the self-hater does not always see that), and I didn't have to feel so ashamed of my depression and despair that I tried to hide them. For until then I'd been such a good pretender; the overdose and sudden descent into insomnia, truancy, compulsive eating and loss of faith took everyone by surprise; even me. Until then I'd been head girl, super-efficient

Saturday salesgirl, visitor of old ladies with Task Force, religiously questioning but still devout, had plenty of friends, told lots of jokes, was reasonable-looking; only the scabs in my ears and on my scalp should have been a giveaway.

Attempted suicide, I once read, represents a desperate and slightly lazy way to be reborn. It's the way you take when your courage fails you, when you know you want more than your present life offers, but not how to find it. There's a kind of twisted optimism to it; hey, stop this world, I want to get off!

But it isn't the best way. Today, when I think of the good things in my life, I feel a kind of awe; what if I hadn't made it, if I hadn't stuck around? What of all the good experiences I would have missed, and all the good people, who showed me that love and loyalty and trust are possible and sometimes, even if only momentarily, wholeness; what Wordsworth called 'intimations of immortality'; those dizzying blessed moments when making love, giving birth, dancing, or sometimes humbly just hanging out washing, when time stops, and the painful gap between one's mind and body and whatever one calls God, nature, vanishes, to be replaced by unity, purpose, the joy of being part of the miracle of life on earth; for once, in harmony.

Yes, those moments are worth hanging around for, even if it is hard to stay in touch with what they teach us during times when the sheer aggro of everyday life gets us down. But if there is one thing I've learnt, am still learning, as I get older, it is that things change. Nothing stays the same for ever. Just around the corner, if only you can sit out this miserable time, may be that transforming moment, person or insight you've been looking for.

But the strange thing is, half the time you don't at first even recognise them, know them for what they are. Aged eighteen, and working as an interviewer in an employment agency because I was convinced I'd failed my A levels (well, I didn't even turn up for one of them), I met Judi. This colleague, five years older than I, gave me R. D. Laing's electrifying *Sanity, Madness and the Family* to read, which freed me further from self-blame, and in the years following stood by me, still loved me, when I erupted from self-hatred into other-hatred – hatred, it sometimes seemed, of anyone who hadn't had it as tough as me; a seething ball of bitter anger; a necessary stage to recovery, perhaps, but not a pleasant thing to witness or be on the receiving end of, as she, friend of so many years now, sometimes was. Did I recognise my meeting her as a transforming moment? No, not at all; in fact I loathed her, because she had such a posh accent; she became my friend in spite of me.

Which is just as well, for this Jew influenced by Buddhism, met in the unlikely setting of a testing ground in women's shorthand and typing skills, handed me, with my guilt-ridden but still spiritually hungry 'ex'-Catholic's soul, the astonishing notion that God might be in all of us: something which stayed with me, even during the years of my professed atheism. Just as important, she airily assured me that one day I would be a published writer, and I wondered how she had guessed my secret ambition; she believed in me long before I, of whom my father demanded of my teachers at parents' evenings, 'Well, is there any hope for It?' dared to believe in myself.

Other transforming moments: leaving a boyfriend when, to my amazement, I got that university place; realising that if I was expected to 'choose' between him or education, I would choose for me – not flee at eighteen, like so many unhappy girls I knew, into the arms of the first man to offer bed and board, shacking up or marriage, a gilt-covered cage to save me from the terrifying task of finding and defining myself; not just so-and-so's daughter, now so-and-so's wife, but Eileen, *me*.

And then finding at university not just books and exhilarating ideas and dancing till the small hours, between wonderful let's-change-the-world late-night arrogance, but Dr Forster; lovely man, creative healer, and years later still my friend, who at last provided the regular, in-depth therapy I'd been craving, showing me that some men could care, some men could listen and even say 'safe journey' as I, like so many young women at the start of the seventies, with great excitement, discovered and helped to create this century's second wave of feminism.

Back then, in 1972, few books, magazines or television documentaries admitted that anything might be painful about women's lives. With what bated breath we listened in our consciousness-raising sessions to other women describe their lives, *our* lives; realised there were so many dumped on daughters, victimised mothers, girls whose ambitions were scorned, dignity and hymens torn, stuffing themselves with food because they were so emotionally hungry, or starving themselves because they felt they deserved so little. So much female pain – not an easy thing to face, but in its own way the discovery was heady; for it meant you were no longer alone, either in suffering or in choosing to rebel, to survive; and it was another way, too, of realising that you weren't to blame, A Bad Girl who somehow deserved whatever life and Daddy dished out to her. With the discovery that so many women and children were abused, oppressed, we finally realised that it wasn't *we* who were out of synch, but a world top-heavy with masculine power and values.

Why am I writing such things, and how can I put my name to them? Were my mother still alive, I wouldn't. It hurt her so much knowing that her children were unhappy. I feel some guilt towards my father about this less than flattering portrait. He does have his good sides and his excuses; a farm labourer's son who couldn't take up a grammar school scholarship because the uniform cost too much, and his family needed him out working, his working life must have been one of frustration. Probably I, the surrogate son who did make it to grammar school, exacerbated that, for I rapidly fell foul of my convent's snobbier values, felt ashamed of his fondness of bread and dripping for tea and his habit of putting milk on the table in its bottle; my friends' parents used jugs.

Nor can it have been easy to have been married to a woman as mentally fragile as my mother – even if it is debatable which came first, her fragility or his insensitivity. How am I to know what their marriage was like in its earliest years, when its pattern was set?

None the less, I experienced my father as I did, and only finally began to overcome the self-hatred induced by his constant criticism when I realised that whatever I did, I would in his eyes always be wrong. Equally, whatever my needs, I would nearly always be let down by him. I had therefore to give up hoping for his approval and protection, and learn to believe in and look after myself.

It would be nice to report that my mother ceased to be a victim, stopped chopping her hair, cheerful things like that. But life ain't that simple. My mother did eventually divorce my father and find some kind of peace, albeit a humble one, in the two-roomed caravan that was the only home she could afford. But a life that had been so hard from the word go left its scars. Motherless at ten days old, as a small child in the hungry thirties she hawked firewood around the street and sang for pennies in a Glasgow shipyard. Aged twelve she sailed back alone from wartime exile in Derry in order to bury her father, when he was found murdered. All that, then marriage to our father, left her so hungry for love that we, her daughters, never really knew whether we were her mother or she ours; and when she died, with each of us around her bed, bound by both enormous love and enormous guilt, she was still wearing a wig to cover up where she had chopped, chopped, chopped her hair, even when terminally ill. Punishing herself for God knows what imagined sins.

I tell this story also to illustrate something else that is so hard to accept when a parent whom you love very much is in great need: you cannot rescue anyone else in this life. You can offer them a helping hand, but you can't do it for them. All you can do is rescue yourself. That is your responsibility and possibility.

That one I didn't realise in any grand flash of a transforming moment either. It was only really my mother's death that finally freed me from guilt at my inability to rescue her. Still, I started along that road, aged sixteen, when the lady at Release said, 'Why do you hate yourself so much? And who has made you?'; Dad, who found it convenient for his daughters to be self-hating; and Mum, poor Mum, who couldn't but teach self-hate through her own scissor-wielding example.

But Mum taught me something else, too: the wonder of laughter as a way of coping with pain, recognising the double-sidedness of life, or simply having fun. On her last night I slept in the same bed with her, this woman who died too young, and in the small hours I woke to find her turn a grimace into a grin, and banter, in her broadest accent, 'Och, Eileen, ah'm all flittery-fluttery in ma wee tummy.' That was her jokey way of saying the cancer hurt, she needed morphine, and they were her last words before her sleep became the final coma.

Humour heals, and in my case it was my mother's greatest gift to me. In all of us, even the most wounded, there is some kernel of strength, of well-ness; the point is, how can we tap into it? Perhaps some people can never remember being happy as children, but I at least can recall being cheerful and delighted with life until the age of seven, when my younger sister was born and my mother first tripped into the abyss from which she never really returned. Through meditation and self-hypnosis, easy to learn but startlingly effective, I have learnt how to refind that younger Eileen, she of the still healthy mother and loving self-image, and, too, to greet all the sad, scabby, suicidal Eileens who followed, to rescue them from whatever part of my brain their pain is still imprinted in, and give them reassurance: Look, it's all right – we made it through!

No experience need be wasted, purposeless; the point is, how can we get through it, who can help us, and what can we learn from it? For me, aged sixteen and a secret hoarder of death-bringing pills, asking those questions was indeed a moment of transformation, for they helped me to save my own life.

# SALLY MORGAN

......................................

## *Grandmother's Secret*

Sally Morgan was born in Perth, Western Australia, in 1951.
She completed a Bachelor of Arts degree at the University of
Western Australia in 1974. She has postgraduate diplomas in
counselling psychology and computing and library studies. She has
established a reputation as an artist, with works in many private
collections and in the Australian National Gallery in Canberra.

She has written an autobiography, My Place, about her
background, including the stories of her great-uncle, mother and
grandmother. She is now writing her second book. She is married
and has three children.

'Grandmother's Secret' is taken from My Place, (Virago 1988).

......................................

On the fourteenth of February, 1966, Australia's currency
changed from pounds, shillings and pence to dollars and cents.
According to Mum and Nan, it was a step backwards in our
history. 'There's no money like the old money,' Nan main-
tained, and Mum agreed. They had both been shocked when
they heard that our new money would not have as much silver
in it as the old two-shilling, one-shilling, sixpence and three-
pence. They influenced my views to such an extent that when
we were given a free choice for our creative writing essay at
school, I wrote a long paper on how the country was going to
rack and ruin because we were changing our money.

'It'll go bad, Glad,' said Nan one night, 'you wait and see.
You can't make money like that, it'll turn green.'

Then I noticed that Nan had a jar on the shelf in the kitchen
with a handful of two-shilling pieces in it. Towards the end of
the week the jar was overflowing with sixpences, threepences,

one-shilling and two-shilling pieces. I could contain my curiosity no longer.

'What are you saving up for, Nan?'

'Nothin'! Don't you touch any of that money!'

I cornered Mum in the bath. 'Okay Mum, why is Nan hoarding all that money? You're supposed to hand it over to the bank and get new money.'

'Don't you say anything to anyone about that money, Sally.'

'Why not?'

'Look, that money's going to be valuable one day, we're saving it for you kids. When it's worth a lot, we'll sell it and you kids can have what we make. You might need it by then.'

I went back in the kitchen and said to Nan, 'Mum told me what you're up to. I think it's crazy.'

'Hmph! We don't care what you think, you'll be glad of it in a few years' time. Now you listen, if anyone from the government comes round asking for money, you tell them we gave all ours to the bank. If they pester you about the old money, you just say you don't know nothin'. You tell 'em we haven't got money like that in this house.'

'Nan,' I half laughed, 'no one from the government is gunna come round and do that!'

'Ooh, don't you believe it. You don't know what the government's like, you're too young. You'll find out one day what they can do to people. You never trust anybody who works for the government, you dunno what they say about you behind your back. You mark my words, Sally.'

I was often puzzled by the way Mum and Nan approached anyone in authority; it was as if they were frightened. I knew that couldn't be the reason – why on earth would anyone be frightened of the government?

Apart from art and English, I failed everything else in the second term of my third year in high school. And Mum was disgusted with my seven per cent for geometry and trigonometry.

'You've got your Junior, soon. How on earth do you expect to pass that?'

'I don't care whether I pass or not. Why don't you let me leave school?'

'You'll leave school over my dead body!'

'What's the point in all this education if I'm going to spend the rest of my life drawing and painting?'

'You are not going to spend the rest of your life doing that, there's no future in it. Artists only make money after they're dead and gone.'

'Suits me.'

I gave up arguing and retreated to my room. Mum never took my ambition to be an artist seriously. Not that she didn't encourage me to draw. Once, when I was bored, she had let me paint pictures all over the asbestos sheets that covered in our back veranda. Nan had thought it was real good: 'Better than getting the housing to do it.'

I sighed. Nan believed in my drawings.

The following weekend, my Aunty Judy came to lunch. She was a friend of Mum's. Her family, the Drake-Brockmans, and ours had known each other for years. 'Sally, I want to have a talk with you about your future,' she said quietly, after we'd finished dessert.

I glared at Mum.

'You know you can't be an artist. They don't get anywhere in this world. You shouldn't worry your mother like that. She wants you to stay at school and finish your Leaving. You can give up all idea of art school because it's just not on!'

I was absolutely furious. Not because of anything Aunty Judy had said, but because Mum had the nerve to get someone from outside the family to speak to me. Mum walked around looking guilty for the rest of the afternoon.

It wasn't only Mum and Aunty Judy, it was my art teacher at

school as well. He held up one of my drawings in front of the class one day and pointed out everything wrong with it. There was no perspective, I was the only one with no horizon line. My people were flat and floating. You had to turn it on the side to see what half the picture was about. On and on he went. By the end of ten minutes, the whole class was laughing and I felt very small. I had always believed that drawing was my only talent; now I knew I was no good at that, either.

The thought of that horrible day made me want to cry. I was glad I was in my room and on my own, because I suddenly felt tears rushing to my eyes and spilling down my cheeks. I decided then to give up drawing. I was sick of banging my head against a brick wall. I got together my collection of drawings and paintings, sneaked down to the back of the yard, and burnt them.

When Mum and Nan found out what I'd done, they were horrified. 'All those beautiful pictures,' Nan moaned, 'gone for ever.' Mum just glared at me. I knew she felt she couldn't say too much – after all, she was partly responsible for driving me to it.

It took about a month for Mum and me to make up. She insisted that if I did my Junior, she wouldn't necessarily make me go on to my Leaving. I, like a fool, believed her.

Towards the end of the school year, I arrived home early one day to find Nan sitting at the kitchen table, crying. I froze in the doorway, I'd never seen her cry before.

'Nan . . . what's wrong?'

'Nothin'!'

'Then what are you crying for?'

She lifted up her arm and thumped her clenched fist hard on the kitchen table. 'You bloody kids don't want me, you want a bloody white grandmother, I'm Black. Do you hear, Black, Black, Black!' With that, Nan pushed back her chair and hurried out to her room. I continued to stand in the doorway, I could feel the strap of my heavy schoolbag cutting into my shoulder, but I was too stunned to remove it.

For the first time in my fifteen years, I was conscious of Nan's colouring. She was right, she wasn't white. Well, I thought logically, if she wasn't white, then neither were we. What did that make us, what did that make me? I had never thought of myself as being Black before.

That night, as Jill and I were lying quietly on our beds, looking at a poster of John, Paul, George and Ringo, I said, 'Jill . . . did you know Nan was Black?'

'Course I did.'

'I didn't, I just found out.'

'I know you didn't. You're really dumb, sometimes. God, you reckon I'm gullible, some things you just don't see.'

'Oh . . .'

'You know we're not Indian, don't you?' Jill mumbled.

'Mum said we're Indian.'

'Look at Nan, does she look Indian?'

'I've never really thought about how she looks. Maybe she comes from some Indian tribe we don't know about.'

'Ha! That'll be the day! You know what we are, don't you?'

'No, what?'

'Boongs, we're Boongs!' I could see Jill was unhappy with the idea.

It took a few minutes before I summoned up enough courage to say, 'What's a Boong?'

'A Boong. You know, Aboriginal. God, of all things, we're Aboriginal!'

'Oh.' I suddenly understood. There was a great deal of stigma attached to being Aboriginal at our school.

'I can't believe you've never heard the word Boong,' she muttered in disgust. 'Haven't you ever listened to the kids at school? If they want to run you down, they say, "Aah, ya just a Boong." Honestly, Sally, you live the whole of your life in a daze!'

Jill was right, I did live in a world of my own. She was much more attuned to our social environment. It was important for her to be accepted at school because she enjoyed being there. All I wanted to do was stay home.

'You know, Jill,' I said after a while, 'if we are Boongs, and I don't know if we are or not, but if we are, there's nothing we can do about it, so we might as well just accept it.'

'Accept it? Can you tell me one good thing about being an Abo?'

'Well, I don't know much about them,' I answered. 'They like animals, don't they? We like animals.'

'A lot of people like animals, Sally. Haven't you heard of the RSPCA?'

'Of course I have! But don't Abos feel close to the earth and all that stuff?'

'God, I don't know. All I know is none of my friends like them. You know, I've been trying to convince Lee for two years that we're Indian.' Lee was Jill's best friend and her opinions were very important. Lee loved Nan, so I didn't see that it mattered.

'You know Susan?' Jill said, interrupting my thoughts. 'Her mother said she doesn't want her mixing with you because you're a bad influence. She reckons all Abos are a bad influence.'

'Aaah, I don't care about Susan, never liked her much anyway.'

'You still don't understand, do you,' Jill groaned in disbelief. 'It's a terrible thing to be Aboriginal. Nobody wants to know you, not just Susan. You can be Indian, Dutch, Italian, anything, but not Aboriginal! I suppose it's all right for someone like you, you don't care what people think. You don't need anyone, but I do!' Jill pulled her rugs over her head and pretended she'd gone to sleep. I think she was crying, but I had too much new information to think about to try and comfort her. Besides, what could I say?

Nan's outburst over her colouring and Jill's assertion that we were Aboriginal heralded a new phase in my relationship with my mother. I began to pester her incessantly about our background. Mum was a hard nut to crack and consistently denied Jill's assertion. She even told me that Nan had come out on a boat from India in the early days. In fact, she was so convincing I began to wonder if Jill was right after all.

When I wasn't pestering Mum, I was busy pestering Nan. To my surprise, I discovered that Nan had a real short fuse when it came to talking about the past. Whenever I attempted to question her, she either lost her temper and began to accuse me of all sorts of things, or she locked herself in her room and wouldn't emerge until it was time for Mum to come home from work. It was a conspiracy.

One night, Mum came into my room and sat on the end of my bed. She had her This Is Serious look on her face. With an unusual amount of firmness in her voice, she said quietly, 'Sally, I want to talk to you.'

I lowered my *Archie* comic. 'What is it?'

'I think you know, don't act dumb with me. You're not to bother Nan any more. She's not as young as she used to be and your questions are making her sick. She never knows when you're going to try and trick her. There's no point in digging up the past, some things are better left buried. Do you understand what I'm saying? You're to leave her alone.'

'Okay, Mum,' I replied glibly, 'but on one condition.'

'What's that?'

'You answer one question for me?'

'What is it?' Poor Mum, she was a trusting soul.

'Are we Aboriginal?'

Mum snorted in anger and stormed out. Jill chuckled from her bed. 'I don't know why you keep it up. Why keep pestering them? I think it's better not to know for sure, that way you don't have to face up to it.'

'I keep pestering them because I want to know the truth, and I want to hear it from Mum's own lips.'

'It's a lost cause, they'll never tell you.'

'I'll crack 'em one day.'

Jill shrugged good-naturedly and went back to reading her *True Romance* magazine.

I settled back into my mattress and began to think about the past. Were we Aboriginal? I sighed and closed my eyes. A mental picture flashed vividly before me. I was a little girl again, and Nan and I were squatting in the sand near the back steps.

'This is a track, Sally. See how they go.' I watched, entranced, as she made the pattern of a kangaroo. 'Now, this is a goanna and here are emu tracks. You see, they're all different. You got to know all of them if you want to catch tucker.'

'That's real good, Nan.'

'You want me to draw you a picture, Sal?' she said as she picked up a stick.

'Okay.'

'These are men, you see, three men. They are very quiet, they're hunting. Here are kangaroos, they're listening, waiting. They'll take off if they know you're coming.' Nan wiped the sand picture out with her hand. 'It's your turn now,' she said, 'you draw something.' I grasped the stick eagerly.

'This is Jill and this is me. We're going down the swamp.' I drew some trees and bushes.

I opened my eyes and, just as suddenly, the picture vanished. Had I remembered something important? I didn't know. That was the trouble, I knew nothing about Aboriginal people. I was clutching at straws.

It wasn't long before I was too caught up in my preparations for my Junior examinations to bother too much about where we'd come from. At that time, the Junior exam was the first major one in high school, and to a large extent, it determined your future. If you failed, you automatically left school and looked for a job. If you passed, it was generally accepted that you would do another two years' study and aim at entrance to university.

Mum was keen on me doing well, so I decided that for her, I'd make the effort and try and pass subjects I'd previously failed. For the first time in my school life, I actually sat up late, studying my textbooks. It was hard work, but Mum encouraged me by bringing in cups of tea and cake or toast and jam.

After each examination, she'd ask me anxiously how I'd gone. My reply was always 'Okay'. I never really knew. Sometimes, I thought I'd done all right, but then I reasoned that all I needed was a hard marker and I might fail. I didn't want to get Mum's hopes up.

Much to the surprise of the whole family, I passed every subject, even scoring close to the distinction mark in English and art. Mum was elated.

'Now, aren't you pleased? I knew you could do it. Mr Buddee was right about you.'

Good old Mr Buddee. I didn't know whether to curse or thank him. Now that I had passed my Junior, I sensed that there was no hope of Mum allowing me to leave school. I should have deliberately failed, I thought. Then she wouldn't have had any choice. Actually, I had considered doing just that, but for some reason I couldn't bring myself to do it. I guess it was my pride again.

Fourth-year high school was different to third-year. It was supposed to be a transitory year where we were treated more like adults and less like difficult teenagers. Even our classes were supposed to be structured to mimic the kind of organisation we might find later in tertiary institutions. I was a year older, but I was still the same person with the same problems. I felt this was also true of school. The changes were only superficial. However, some deep and important things did happen to me that year.

One day, I happened to bump into a girl whom I'd been

friendly with in my Sunday school days. She invited me to a youth meeting to be held at a nearby church hall.

'Aw, no thanks, Sharon. I won't come.'

'Look, it's not going to be anything like you might imagine,' she said confidently. 'Nothing to do with religion, just some Chinese food and a bit of a get-together, that's all.'

'You sure?'

'Positive.'

'Okay, I'll come. I know some other kids who like Chinese food. I might bring them too.'

'Great. See you there.'

I arrived at the meeting with seven girls from around our neighbourhood and two from school. The food was quite good, and even though everyone else there ignored us, we enjoyed ourselves. When everyone had finished stuffing themselves, a chap stood up and said, 'We have a Mr McClean here to give us a little talk. I'd like you all to be quiet while we listen to what he has to say.'

Uh-oh, I thought. Here it comes. I looked towards the back of the hall; the door was closed and there were two elderly gentlemen standing in front of it. I was trapped. I could feel my insides twisting themselves into a knot. I knew if Mr McClean turned out to be half as boring as some of the teachers I'd had in Sunday school, my friends would never forgive me.

Mr McClean stood up and smiled nicely at us all. 'I'm here to talk to all you young people about your future,' he said. Your eternal future, I mouthed quietly in unison with Mr McClean. I'd heard it all before. It was going to be a long night.

As he continued, I began to think of other things, like the new clothes Mum had promised to buy me, the latest quiz show on television and the way Jill seemed to be able to whip up an outfit on our old treadle machine in no time at all.

Suddenly, there was someone talking to me. I knew it wasn't Mr McClean. I looked around in a furtive kind of way, trying to see who it was. All eyes were fixed on the speaker, there was no one new in the room.

'Who are you?' I asked mentally.

With a sudden dreadful insight, I knew it was God.

'What are you doing here?' I asked. I don't know why I was surprised. It was a church hall, after all.

It had to be Him because the voice seemed to come from without, not within; it transcended the reality of the room. I couldn't even see my surroundings any more. I was having an audience with Him, whom I dreaded. The mental images that I had built up of Him so far in my life began to dissolve, and in their place came a new image. A person, overwhelming love, acceptance and humour. What Nan'd call real class. In an instant, I became what others refer to as a believer.

I joined the local youth group after that. I was full of ideas for making the meetings and outings we went on more interesting, but it was difficult to change the pattern that had been set in motion so many years before. I became friendly with a girl a few years older than me. She was reasonably conservative, but less so than the other girls I'd met, and she had an excellent sense of humour. I could never understand why a lot of the girls at church considered cracking jokes unladylike. Thank heavens Pat wasn't like that.

One day, she said to me, 'You know, no one here can figure out why you like youth group so much, but hate church. What's the difference?'

In Pat's eyes, one was a natural extension of the other, but to me, church was practically the antipathy of youth group. I always felt uncomfortable in church, it was so formal and lacking in spontaneity. The sermons were full of clichés and things I didn't understand. To me, church was like school, more concerned with red tape than with the guts of the matter.

I think Mum was relieved that I was finally channelling my energies into what she saw as something creative. Up until then, she hadn't been sure how I'd turn out. Now she hoped that, with the encouragement of people at church, I would begin to lead a more productive and less rebellious life. She was wrong.

One night, one of the deacons of the church asked if he could talk to me. I was friendly with his daughter and he seemed like a nice man, so I agreed.

'You and Mary are having quite a lot to do with one another, aren't you?' he asked.

'I suppose so, but we're not best friends.'

'No, I know that, but you see a lot of each other at youth group and church.'

'Yeah.'

'Well, Sally,' he smiled, 'I want to ask a favour of you.'

'Sure, anything.'

'I'd like you to stop mixing with Mary.' He smiled his charming smile again.

'Why?' I was genuinely puzzled.

'I think you know why.'

'No, I don't.'

'You're a bad influence, you must realise that.' Believe it or not, that was one part of my character I was unaware of.

'What do you mean?' I wanted him to spell it out.

'This is Mary's Leaving year, the same as yours. I don't want her mixing with you in case she picks up any of your bad habits.'

Aaah, I thought. He's heard about my truancy.

'What about after Leaving?' I asked meekly. I sensed there was more to this than just that.

'No. I don't think so. Really, it'd be better if you broke off your friendship entirely. You do understand, don't you?' he said in an incredibly charming way.

'Oh, I understand,' I replied. I was amazed that he could have such a charming manner and yet be such a dag.

'Good girl, I knew you would.' He was relieved. 'Oh, by the way. I can count on you not to say anything to Mary, can't I?

You'll find a way of breaking things off between you, won't you?'

I nodded my head, and he walked off.

I was hurt and disappointed. He was a deacon, I'd looked up to him. I was lucky I had my pride, it came to my rescue yet again. I didn't need people like him, I decided.

It was about that time that I began to analyse my own attitudes and feelings more closely. I looked at Mum and Nan and I realised that part of my inability to deal constructively with people in authority had come from them. They were completely baffled by the workings of government or its bureaucracies. Whenever there were difficulties, rather than tackle the system directly, they'd taught us it was much more effective to circumvent or forestall it. And if that didn't work, you could always ignore it.

That summer, the state housing decided to paint the exterior of all the houses in our street – a decision that really panicked Nan. She made sure the front and back doors were kept locked so they couldn't come inside, and she spent most of the day peeping out at them from behind the curtains.

I tried to reason with her, but to no avail. The fact that state housing employees had only ever called to collect the rent or carry out routine maintenance meant nothing to Nan. For her, they were here to check on us, and the possibility of eviction was always there, hanging over our heads like some invisible guillotine.

I thought back to all the years she had spent buttering up the rent men. Each rent day, Nan would go through the same routine. She rose early and spent all morning cleaning the house – not that she ever intended letting the rent man in. It was just a way of relieving all her nervous tension. Then she washed and dried our best cup and saucer and arranged a plate of biscuits in tempting display. After that, she hunted for a milk jug that didn't have a crack in it. Her final touch was to plump up the cushion we had sitting on the chair on the front porch. She wanted him to be comfortable.

And the whole time Nan was preparing morning tea, she'd grumble under her breath: 'That bloody rent man! Who does he think he is, taking up my time like this? Doesn't he know I've got work to do?' Of course, once he arrived it was a different story.

'You're here at last,' she'd smile, 'sit down, you must be tired. They shouldn't make you walk so far.'

Why did she do it? I asked myself. Why was she afraid? It was a free country, wasn't it? I decided I'd try and talk to her again. Try to explain how things worked.

After Nan had given the painters a slap-up morning tea, I cornered her out the back, where she was raking up leaves. 'Nan,' I said suspiciously, 'I think I've just realised why you've been treating the rent man like royalty all these years. You've been bribing them, haven't you?'

'I don't know what you're talking about, Sally.'

'Yes, you do. All these years, you've been frightened that we'd get evicted. That's why you've been buttering up the rent man. You thought if it came to the crunch, he might put in a good word for us.'

'Good men have collected rent from this house over the years, Sally. Don't you go running down the rent men.'

'You know I'm not running down the rent men, Nan, I'm just trying to talk about all this.'

'Talk, talk, talk, that's all you do. You don't do any work.'

'Nan,' I said, in a reasonable tone of voice, 'I don't think you understand about the house we rent.'

'What do you mean?' she muttered as she kept her head down and continued to rake.

'Well, you only get evicted if you don't look after the place. For example, if we were to smash a wall or break all the windows, they might think about throwing us all out, but otherwise, as long as we pay the rent, they let you stay.'

'Hmmph, you think you know everything, don't you?' she replied bitterly. 'You don't know nothin', girl. You don't know what it's like for people like us. We're like those Jews, we got to look out for ourselves.'

'What do you mean, people like us? We're just like anybody else, aren't we? I didn't even know you knew Jews existed, how on earth could we be the same as them?'

'In this world there's no justice; people like us'd all be dead and gone now if it was up to this country.' She stopped and wiped her mouth with a man's handkerchief. Her eyes looked tired and wet.

'Nan,' I said carefully. 'What people are we?'

She was immediately on the defensive. She looked sharply at me with the look of a rabbit sensing danger. 'You're tryin' to trick me again. Aaah, you can't be trusted. I'm not stupid, you know. I'm not saying nothing. Nothing, do you hear.'

I suddenly felt terribly sad. The barriers were up again. Just when I thought I was finally getting somewhere. 'Nan,' I coaxed, 'I'm not trying to trick you. I just want to know what people we are, that's all.'

'I'm not talking, I'm not talking,' she muttered as she dropped her rake and put her hands over her ears.

I sighed and walked back to the house. Inside, I felt all churned up, but I didn't know why. I had accepted by now that Nan was dark, and that our heritage was not that shared by most Australians, but I hadn't accepted that we were Aboriginal. I was too ignorant to make such a decision, and too confused. I found myself coming back to the same old question: if Nan was Aboriginal, why didn't she just say so? The fact that Mum and Nan made consistent denials made me think I was barking up the wrong tree. I could see no reason why they would pretend to be something they weren't. And Nan's remark about the Jews had confused me even more. I knew a lot about the Jews because of the war and Dad. In my mind, there was no possible comparison between us and them.

# CLARE BAYLEY

## *Sex and Sexuality*

**C**lare Bayley, born in 1963, spent her childhood in Oxford and
County Durham. Between school and university, she spent six
months in France teaching English in a primary school. Studying
French and Italian at university gave her more opportunities to
work abroad. She now lives in London and is a freelance
journalist.

When I was eighteen I left home and went with a friend to the
heart of rural France to be an *assistante* (an assistant English
teacher). She lived in a pretty, walled town down in the valley,
and I lived in a bleak, ugly town on top of a plateau, half an
hour away from her by train. There were four trains a day, two
going north to Paris and two going south to Spain. On Wednes-
days, when there were no classes, and every weekend we would
take the appropriate train north or south, and visit each other.
The rest of the time I spent completely alone in my room next
to the girls' dormitory, except for Tuesday evenings, when I
went to a drama group. One of the teachers at my school put me
in touch with a man called Gérard, who was directing the play.
The headmaster at my school had warned me about Gérard as
an 'undesirable and a troublemaker' and advised me to avoid
'those kind of people', meaning the Communists.

The teacher took me along to his home one Tuesday evening
to introduce me to Gérard. When I arrived there was a meeting
of the local Communist Party in progress, but I was welcomed
in to sit down. They had nearly finished, and Gérard should be
arriving soon. He's always late for everything, he's an *artist*,
they explained indulgently. I had my back to the door. When

Gérard walked in all conversations stopped, there was a palpable air of expectancy and all eyes turned smiling towards the door. Gérard swept into the room, slamming the door behind him, and with a flamboyant gesture stubbed out his cigarette in a saucer. He was evidently in a bad temper, but acknowledged the gestures of welcome with tired magnanimity. He said he had just been to the printers' to pick up some posters; that was why he was late. When he was introduced to me, he dismissed the moment and me with an impatient gesture and turned straight to the weightier matter of the posters. His offhandedness seemed calculatedly rude, and I was disproportionately angry.

He continued to ignore me, and talk animatedly to the comrades. I sat smoking crossly, feeling embarrassed to be there and unsure whether he would even agree to take me to the rehearsal. Then, without interrupting his conversation, he leaned across, took a cigarette out of my packet with an insolent gesture and, without ever looking at me, lit up. I pretended not to notice, but a little while later I leaned across the table and calmly took a cigarette out of his packet. He noticed and looked at me rather sharply, so I smiled sweetly and lit up. His challenge had been taken up.

From that Tuesday on, Gérard picked me up from the school each week to give me a lift to rehearsals. I knew he was thirty-four and married, but I began to be addicted to the ten minutes per week we spent alone in the car together: it was the only really intimate contact I had with anyone in the village. For those ten minutes he would drop his veneer of constant mockery and provocation. He would be gentle and sad and considerate and tell me stories about his past: how he had worked as a toreador at the bullring in Nîmes, and been kicked out of art school, and gone drinking with Henry Moore in little bars in the backstreets. He told me things that I thought he didn't tell anyone else. His paintings decorated the walls of many of the bars in the village, and they were all of sad clowns. Whenever I saw them I felt as if I had a special insight into them.

All through the winter it was bitterly cold with snow on the ground, and the villagers were suspicious of me and spoke in patois, or French so heavily accented I could barely understand. They called wine *'vaing'* instead of *'vin'* and referred to my job as *'assistentez'* instead of *'assistante'*. They never seemed to know my name, but addressed me as *'l'assistentez d'ainglez'*, the English assistant.

Slowly I began to meet other teachers who were sympathetic. Many of them lived two hundred kilometres south, in Montpellier, and went back there almost every weekend. They offered me lifts down to Montpellier and sometimes invited me to stay with them. Even when it was snowing in the mountains, in Montpellier people were walking around in shirt sleeves and the mimosa was in bloom on all the trees, making the whole town fragrant. My friend and I began to strike out from Montpellier, hitching to nearby towns like Nîmes and Carcassonne and Toulouse. I travelled in a big, tough coat with gold buttons and a small Turkish bag slung over my shoulder which contained everything I needed. I felt completely free, and ready for adventures.

I began to love France, and to love having my own room and my own life. My older sister had always gone on about the need for autonomy, so I had always dared myself to sit reading on my own in cafés. But now I found that I really enjoyed doing that, and not just as a pose. I had croissants for breakfast, and every morning when the *boulanger* greeted me as 'the English girl', saying *'Bonjour, Mademoiselle l'Anglaise'*, it no longer seemed like an insult, but an affectionate nickname. People began to know who I was, and I started to say *'vaing'* instead of *'vin'*. The butcher was the parent of one of my pupils, as was the woman at the check-out at the supermarket, and when I went to get my work permit the clerk in the town hall already knew all about me because his sister-in-law was a teacher at the school. When spring finally came, the snow melted and all the fields were covered knee-deep in wild daffodils and narcissus which the children picked and sold to perfume companies for three francs a sack. I began to be invited to parties, and then Gérard offered me a part in the play because somebody had dropped out.

My birthday fell on a Tuesday that year. I asked Gérard if I could miss a rehearsal, because I wanted to invite some of my tentative new friends round. He shouted that we had to take this play seriously or it wasn't worth doing at all, and refused to let me take the evening off. On the night of my birthday it was raining hard. Gérard arrived early and I jumped into his car and he roared away without saying a word of greeting. I thought he was still angry with me for asking for a night off. He didn't drive me to the theatre; instead he screeched to a halt in a timber yard on the way.

Without a word he reached into the back of the car and brought out a pile of presents, which he started to stack up on top of me. There were flowers, and pictures he'd done, and a bottle of vodka. I was completely dumbfounded. When I asked for some explanation he said that loving me would never stop him loving his wife. He seemed to think that would clarify everything for me, but it was hardly the reassurance I was looking for.

All through the winter I had never taken my infatuation very seriously. Gérard was wonderful company because anything was possible when you were with him, but even though he flirted with me outrageously I never bothered to think it through as a serious possibility. To be suddenly presented with Gérard as a potential lover was very alarming – it would mean that I would have to have sex with him. It was like going fishing in a stream with a worm on a hook and unexpectedly finding a ten-foot pike on the end of your rod.

Soon after my birthday I went home for two weeks. Gérard made out he was distraught at the prospect of not seeing me for that long, and said there was a 'weekend-theatre' when I got back which I would have to go to at all costs or the play would not be worth putting on. Ever since my birthday I had been thinking a lot about the idea of sleeping with him, and it was beginning to seem a more and more attractive proposition.

On the journey home I exploited my new-found emancipation with indescribable arrogance. The French love nothing better than a young English girl travelling alone, and I conformed absolutely to the role. I charmed the guard into getting me a bunk or *couchette* to sleep in, even though he said he had none left, I sweet-talked the Customs officials, I delighted the fellow passengers, and all the time I thought I was coming out on top. I had never felt so sexy before, and it had gone to my head. To think that men, and men like Gérard, desired me, and that I knew it, and had my own desires, transformed me into an adult, not a child. It seemed to put me on an equal footing with everyone else.

The train journey took twelve hours, and I spent much of that time staring out of the window at the dark French landscape imagining how nice it would be to sleep with Gérard. I felt very wicked and glamorous, and was sure that the other people in the compartment led much duller lives than me. There was a pale and rather spotty boy sitting opposite me who kept staring in what he seemed to think was a suggestive way. If only he knew that someone as exciting and interesting as Gérard had fallen for me, I thought, he wouldn't even bother, and I felt almost sorry for him.

I walked into my mother's home on a cloud of self-satisfaction, and crashed straight into all the old constraints and tensions of family. The first night I had a screaming argument with my older sister about feminism. We were doing the washing-up together and she asked me why I was wearing short skirts and make-up, and questioned me altogether too closely about why I spent so much energy on making myself attractive to men. When she said it was all a conspiracy and I was part of it, I thought she had gone too far. At the time, I was drying a colander, which I threw down on the ground in a furious gesture which seemed very French, and shouted at the top of my voice:

'IF I WANT TO WEAR SHORT SKIRTS THERE'S NO REASON WHY I SHOULDN'T – DON'T TAKE EVERYTHING SO SERIOUSLY – WHAT'S WRONG WITH BEING ATTRACTIVE TO MEN? IT DOESN'T MATTER – I AM COMPLETELY INDEPENDENT AND I KNOW WHAT I'M DOING AND DON'T TAKE EVERYTHING SO SERIOUSLY, I CAN COPE – IT'S YOU WHO'S MAD.' Then I burst into tears and I couldn't understand why.

I spent the rest of the time stomping around the pavements trying to convince myself that I wasn't going to have an affair with Gérard.

I travelled all night back to France, and arrived as the sun was rising. I knew Gérard was coming to pick me up to take me to the weekend-theatre, and it occurred to me that nobody in my family would know what I was up to until it was too late. I didn't know what the sleeping arrangements were for the weekend, but I knew very well that it was a prime opportunity for us to sleep together. It suddenly seemed rather too real, and I began to think of what my sister would say if she knew, and what his wife would do if she knew. Then I started to worry about contraception and it all seemed like a very bad idea. Just as I was putting on some water to make tea, his car drew up outside my window. There was no doubt in my mind that I would calmly but firmly repel his advances. He walked straight into my room without knocking. The effect of his physical presence was astonishing. Just as all conversations would stop when he walked into a room full of people, so all my resolve fell away when he walked in. Shaking, I flung myself into his arms, and he put on his tender, sad face and murmured blandishments into my ear. I was quite delirious, but he didn't even seem unduly surprised. He told me that he had cancelled the weekend-theatre; instead he was taking me to the South, to a cottage surrounded by apple blossom. And so he did.

We spent an ecstatic weekend together, and I thought the love between me and Gérard was a fabulously rare and precious thing. Every time we slept together I spent the next half day in a state of blissful astonishment. I had slept with a couple of people before, but I had never felt such passion and craving. Every time I had an orgasm I felt I was cocking a snook at all the boring people in the village who would have been so shocked if they'd known what 'Mademoiselle l'Anglaise' was doing in her spare time. I never felt ashamed about how much I wanted Gérard, because the more I did, the happier he seemed to be, so I let myself want him more and more. He used to turn up unexpectedly at my door in the middle of the night and I would welcome him with joy. It didn't matter if I wasn't very good at speaking French, because I was getting really good at having orgasms.

But the romance of that wore off. I began to notice that he only *ever* came to see me in the middle of the night, and always left again two hours later. I could never ring him, or be seen in public with him, or spend a whole night with him, or talk about him to anyone except my poor friend, who heard about nothing else.

I was terrified of being found out by the village, which would have ostracised me. When I questioned him about what was going on, he responded by playing me and my fears off against each other. He reminded me what a disaster it would be if his wife found out, and then he would cajole me round, likening himself to an artichoke: his outside leaves were prickly, but inside his heart was tender and succulent. He told me this on two occasions.

I saw myself as a child, running around the legs of the adults, playing at being one of them and joining in their conversations. When I realised that what I was playing at was real, that I was well and truly involved in the machinations and serious consequences of the adult world, I was panicked and resolved never to see Gérard again. But I just couldn't do it.

Gérard was very articulate, and very hard to argue with. He was a man of high political principle, but his analysis of the emancipation of women didn't go further than supporting their right to go on the pill. He often reminded me that he had never promised that I would be the only person in his life. Finally, in a state of emotional exhaustion and profound confusion, I went away to Montpellier with my friend for a weekend. One long, straight stretch of the road to Montpellier was lined with an avenue of plane trees. On every tree as we drove past was Gérard's face on a poster, with '*VOTEZ COMMUNISTE*' emblazoned below.

We would have had a completely calm, self-contained, intimate together time sitting around in cafés, wandering around markets, lying on grass. But the privacy of our companionship was constantly being invaded and interrupted. Groups of young lads laughed at us, shouting as we walked past; waiters asked if we were English or German or Swedish and wanted to make us talk; even old men in bars said things like 'OK Baby' when we walked in. It was still cold in the mountains, but here the sun was warm and we just wanted to bask in it unnoticed.

One afternoon, everything contrived to build up a feeling of fury. We went to see a film about the life of de Maupassant, who was a womaniser and a great bastard as well as a great writer. We came out of the cinema and walked past a military display which sickened us. I was looking at a shop window, not noticing where I was going, and I walked straight into an off-duty conscript who was deliberately blocking my path. He and his friends laughed and laughed at my confusion and stopped us passing for a few moments. We walked on and tried to regain our composure. But I kept on thinking about that moment, and it wouldn't go out of my head.

We were waiting to cross a road when I turned my head and saw an old, battered, grey Citroën van abandoned in an alley-way. On it somebody had scrawled in chalk an obscene picture of a woman's torso with no head, showing her open legs.

It was as shocking as if I had witnessed a rape – the trivial but profound humiliation of a woman by some laughing, brutal man. Suddenly I was aware for the first time of the violence which lies beneath the surface of so many relations between men and women. All the apparent niceties, the jokes, the teasings, the chat-ups in bars were suddenly undercut by this clarity of vision. Once I had seen it, I saw it everywhere and I felt frightened. And angry.

All the so-called admiration women got from men for having nice legs or a pretty face suddenly seemed to mean no more to them than that crude drawing on a wrecked car bonnet. And then it occurred to me that I meant no more to Gérard than that.

Being sexy and attractive had until then given me a feeling of power and freedom, but now I felt in danger. I was treading a thin line between stirring admiration, and stirring something altogether more sinister. There was no love in that drawing on the car. It didn't matter even if all I was after was sex, too. The balance seemed tipped from the start.

I felt a terrible burden of responsibility coming down on my shoulders, and the uneasy feeling that my life would never be the same again.

Of course I didn't go straight back and end it all with Gérard. Instead I sent him a note saying that I wanted to talk to him. He came as soon as he could, at midnight when I had already gone to bed. I told him very calmly that something had happened that made it impossible for me to see him any more. He rose to the occasion by taking it very seriously, and asked me to explain it to him. I did my best in stumbling French, but in the end it just sounded as if I'd bumped into a soldier, seen a rude drawing on a car, and from it all drawn the conclusion that Gérard was exploiting me and didn't love me. I'm sure he didn't realise what was going on, but to his credit he did realise it was important. He had probably been expecting some kind of outburst some time soon.

He set about trying to explain things from his point of view. I realised that it wasn't really as simple as I'd thought. He said he was hurt because I underrated the depth of his affection for me, and that he didn't like his life any more than I did, and he was so persuasive that after a while I almost ended up feeling sorry for *him*. It wasn't that I didn't still want him, but I didn't want him on those terms, because they made me feel powerless and used. Gérard wasn't exactly setting out to use me, but he was part of a society in which it was normal for women to be used and powerless. If only I could break out of the whole system of inequalities. Unfortunately I did want Gérard, and he wasn't prepared to fight against what served him well, so if I was to have him, I had to collude.

We lay on my bed together smoking French cigarettes and I started to feel better, less melodramatic. And then we made love. I dozed off, and woke to find him putting his boots on ready to leave.

# ALICIA PARTNOY

......................................

## *An Argentinian Diary*

*Alicia Partnoy was born in Argentina in 1955. She was among the 30,000 Argentinians who 'disappeared' after the military junta came to power in 1976. During her three years as a political prisoner her stories and poems were smuggled out of prison and published anonymously. On her release she was forced to leave the country and go to the United States. Since her arrival she has presented testimony on human rights violations in Argentina. Her testimony was quoted in the final report of the Argentinian Commission for the Investigation of Disappearance and helped to bring about the convictions of four junta generals in Buenos Aires.*

*She has written a book,* The Little School, *about her time as a political prisoner. She translates and performs her own poetry. Recently her work was set to music by Sweet Honey in the Rock. She has edited an anthology of writings by women in exile from Central and South America,* You Can't Drown the Fire.

*Alicia Partnoy lives in Washington, DC with her husband Antonio and her daughter Ruth. 'An Argentinian Diary' was written in Washington, DC in autumn, 1988.*

......................................

It has already happened to you. You have heard the most secret of your thoughts in the voice of the wrong person. You know first hand that feeling of ridicule and anger, that certainty of being naked in front of a mocking crowd. Then, you don't need more explanations. I don't have to tell you why I first chopped my diary into a million pieces, only to burn that pile of confetti afterwards.

It happened ten minutes after my brother dropped an 'I must hide my feelings. I must. I cry in loneliness, no one listens' while I was walking through his room on my way to the bathroom. That was the proof I needed. The night before, he had greeted me with a 'Love is a fruit that dodges my teeth', totally out of place. I had thought then that probably it had not been a very original sentence to start with, that maybe I had in turn stolen it from some writer. When it happened for the second time I had to face it, especially as my brother's eyes were bright with amusement. The pile of dirty clothes that I was carrying to wash in the bathroom basin fell from my hands in the middle of my brother's room. I hurried to the drawer where I kept my diary. On page 95 I read: 'I wish he could see in my eyes the need for a word, a caress . . . but no, I must hide my feelings. I must. I cry in loneliness, no one listens.'

To tell the truth, I don't exactly remember what happened. I cannot recall the sentence he had chosen, nor can I swear that it was on page 95 of the notebook I called my diary. It is, however, true that I destroyed it. While doing it I insulted myself for being so stupid, so naive, so . . . But those details are not important any more. I was too upset to remember. I wanted to forget the whole incident, to burn the memory of it with my diary. But the workings of one's mind are surprising. After that day it seems that the lack of a diary prompted me to pack the details that come with the events carefully and store them, with plenty of mothballs, in the attic of my memory. Sometimes they do not remain quietly in the assigned box. They jump all over the place, looking for friends. At other times the label with the date on top of the box blurs. However . . . as far as I'm not scared of remembering, I always manage to find them in that mess. Let me unpack some for you.

*20 April 1972*
..........................................

Dear Diary:
    I don't know how to start telling you this, but I have to talk. Tomorrow I'll be too upset with Olga and Lidia to tell them

anything. I know they didn't mean it, but . . . Well, things went like this:

At noon he came to pick me up at the corner where we always meet. He was going to walk me to school like every day. We had a little discussion, but things did not seem to be getting fixed as we were approaching the school. Five more minutes and I had to be in there: maths class, and then geography, and then . . . I decided not to go to school, so we could talk. We had gone over and over that issue of the 'lack of communication'. But when to communicate? Suddenly I felt that I wanted to share all my life with him, but I didn't even know how he felt about a whole lot of things. 'Let's talk,' I said, 'I'll stay with you today.' He was happy.

First we went to the park and we talked and walked. Then we went to his house for hot chocolate and *buñuelos*. His mum wouldn't let me stop eating. He said he wanted to show me something. We went upstairs, to his room, for kisses. He locked the door. I love it when he locks the door. He wanted to play piano on my ribs. I let him do it. I wished he could have heard the music of my nipples. Instead, there was a sound of helicopters. 'The university,' we said. I could not think any more, heavy with his kisses, I felt my body almost melting in his hands. Someone knocked at the door. 'Hijo, Alicia, quick! They are looking for you,' his father said.

We didn't ask questions. He unlocked the door and went after his father. As soon as I could put every single piece of clothing in its proper place, I followed him downstairs. I almost bumped into my mother. How had she found us? She was upset. Oh my, was she upset! Behind the door, almost hiding, were my two friends. This was the story:

My friends had shown my mother the way to the house. Olga and Lidia were dismissed from school very early today because of some kind of strike at the university. They had called me at home to see what was the matter. Was I sick? Why hadn't I attended school? Can you believe it! The first day in my whole life that I decide to skip school without telling . . . Stupid strike! My mother was scared. She had heard on the radio that the students had barricaded themselves into the university, that the police had thrown tear gas at them. She feared that I was with them and that's why they had tracked me down. I was to come back home immediately. The streets were dangerous . . .

Seriously, how could I have been with the students? I don't know what they want. I don't care to know. I want only my freedom. And peace, yes, I want peace. And I want to make love, I really do. I think tomorrow I'll finally tell him 'Yes.'

## 15 October 1972
.............................................

Dear Diary:

You guessed it! I'm again crying in my room. I don't understand them. The grown-ups. They are supposed to know better, so they say. Life will teach me, they say. Life cannot teach me something so crazy. I know I'm right. I'm sure I'm right . . . D'you want to know why I don't wear my David star, why I won't wear it any more? Well, let me go and wash my face and I'll tell you . . .

## 16 October 1972
.............................................

Dear Diary:

Sorry. I never came back to you yesterday. My father tried to talk this issue over while I was coming back from the bathroom. After that, I was too late and I had to write my essay on Cortazar's short story. I like the way he writes. I also like Poe. Anyway, back to my David star. Yesterday Mum found out that I'm going to the church. Worse: that I'm going to two churches! Remember that I go to the youth meetings at this Catholic church near the park? Of course I had never told my parents! I knew they were not going to understand it. I don't go to services, or when I do it's only to be with my friends. I don't know how to sing but I fake it, to be with them in the chorus. My friends and my love. They are all Catholic but they don't try to convert me. I don't know why my parents are so scared. I guess they don't trust me. Adults never trust you. So . . . when they found out about this, and also about my going to the Protestant church, with Sonia . . . you know I go there to play volleyball . . . Well. In a few words: it was a scandal! Such a big deal!

Many years ago they said I was going to have the freedom to choose a religion. I don't want to choose any religion, I just want to be with my friends. And I don't have any Jewish friends. My mother said that one day I may need Jewish friends. She said that if I'm persecuted because of my race, they will be the ones to be with, to protect me. Then I took the David star away from my necklace. I'm not going to wear it any more. After all, the only use of religion is to divide people!


## 20 June 1973

Dear Diary:

We went to the Café today. The eight of us. We always have so much fun together! I guess they are what you call perfect friends. We had lots of coffees and spoke about the political situation. Even though I love to be with them, I didn't want to go. What could I say about the 'situation'? I only knew that I cannot study because of the strikes. All those efforts I made to take the exams so I could skip my last year of high school and go to the university! Then I get there, but there are no classes. Sometimes the classes start and half an hour later all these students come into the class and say: 'We are not having classes today because we will demonstrate in front of the newspaper. Its editorials have been calling for another military *coup*', or 'We cannot have classes because the workers of such-and-such factory are on strike and we'll join them in solidarity', or . . . you know . . .

I didn't dare to say all this at the Café today. Even when I trust my friends as I trust nobody else in the whole world. Somehow I felt it was selfish to think the way I do. Seriously, I realised that I've been extremely selfish. It has been easy to feel pain for those living in poverty or suffering injustice but to do nothing to help them. Today, there was talk of the moments we are living in this country and I guess I'd been too busy to notice. Yes, the first time we have democracy since the year I was born, 1955.

There was talk of literacy campaigns, of helping the people in the shanty towns to get better houses, of discussing the syllabus at school so we could have classes connected to real life . . . It was exciting. You know, what I like a lot is that none of my friends repeats slogans, like so many people at school do. When these friends talk about history it all makes sense. They don't give me a bunch of dates and names. In a way they show me where I come, where my place is in history. Sorry! I'm getting too pretentious. I hardly know how to explain it . . . and I swear it was not all that coffee I had, nor the three cigarettes I smoked . . . I left the Café on O'Higgins' Street feeling that I'm part of a generation that can make things better for all in this country. It's strange, but the word 'politics' doesn't scare me that much any more.


## 24 March 1976

Dear Diary:

I'm glad I destroyed you some years ago. I would have hated to do it today. So many things we'll have to burn today! Books and address books, notes from classes, photographs of our friends in the movement. Today, what we have been fearing for several months finally happened: the military *coup*. The killings have already started and now the military will be able to target more of us. All of us. Before I part with you for this time of danger, let me update you a little.

There have been weddings and births. No time to think of diaries! Of course, I married. My baby girl is nine months old now. I won't tell you about her because it would take me hours. Let me just say that she is one of the reasons for my strong commitment to change things in this country, even with the military here, even now. I don't want my girl to grow up in a repressive, unfair society. Mary and Néstor also had a baby, and Mary is pregnant again! Well, to be brief, the eight of us married. Now we are four formal families. Granted, not so 'formal' . . . The eight of us continued working with the Young Peronists, for social change. Our friends work a lot in the liberation theology movement also. Now I'll have to see them less. We'll probably have to go into hiding. Who knows!

Last month I turned twenty-one. I'm afraid I'll never reach twenty-five. But I'm not sorry for myself; my work will yield its fruits even if I cannot see them. Now let me say goodbye. The matches are waiting. The task is heavy.

Always,
Alicia

Mary and Néstor were kidnapped by the military in November 1976, and disappeared for ever after enduring months of torture. My husband and I were kidnapped and jailed for three years. Our daughter joined us in December 1979, when we were forced to leave the country. We divorced.

The other two couples suffered years of repression but managed not to be arrested.

The poems I had written were also confiscated by the military and used to interrogate my husband during his torture sessions.

We, the survivors, still work for justice and social change.

# JULIA ROBERTSON

## *Out of the Well of Loneliness*

*Julia Robertson was born in 1943 and grew up in New Hampshire. After graduating from university on the west coast of the USA she came to London, lured by the 'swinging sixties', and began working in films. She hadn't planned to stay for ever, but feminism and the friendships that have come out of the women's movement have kept her here.*

'Your daddy's rich and your mama's good-looking . . .' From an early age I knew that refrain and felt its comfort, for I grew up in a world that appeared safe, secure, untroubled. My father was a lawyer – huge, comforting, patient – and my mother was beautiful, attentive to my sister and brother and me, often fun, and certainly mercurial. We owned the first station wagon in our small New Hampshire town and it was always full of children and dogs, being taken skiing, riding, swimming. I was a tomboy and could keep up easily with the boys as we played each day in the woods around us. So I remember my fury at being told by one of them to go home to pee as I couldn't do it outdoors like *them*!

At eight or nine I discovered that I wasn't omnipotent and that was a blow, but survivable: I had lined up all my little friends to watch me throw a stone over a tall house just near ours. The stone hurtled through a huge window that seemed miles below the roof line. But I was saved from punishment by my much-loved grandmother, who arrived that evening, coming down the station platform through the hiss and the steam of the engine, bearing her usual gift – chocolate mice. A mouse instead of a punishment.

Why, then, in those early years did I feel even more powerfully the words that continued the song: 'So hush little baby, don't you cry'? Perhaps even then there were stirrings of the two transforming moments I want to write about – both were times of distress and initial incomprehension. But the first, the death of two people I didn't even know, led to an opening up, a moving outwards; and the second, reading a novel in my mid-teens, to a shutting down of myself in timidity and self-dislike which it took too long to overcome. And that, I can recognise now, was caused by the narrowness and conventionality of the society in which I grew up.

Our small world of privilege had another side to it: it was a ghetto of class and race exclusivity whose unwritten rules and codes of behaviour were thought to be in the blood, so you couldn't go wrong. These codes and rules covered the whole of life besides: no rudeness, no lying, no white shoes for a lady after the first of September, and no velvet before six o'clock in the evening. The confusion in this was that everything, it felt to me, was given exactly the same moral weight. But these were the 1950s, with their rigidities and fears: you allowed a boy to kiss you only after the third date (never mind the notion that you might want to kiss him – I tried it once at twelve and still shiver at the shame of it). And you had to keep an eye out in the school playground in case the Communists arrived in their big, heavy boots, or dropped a bomb, in which case we were trained to run to the windowless school gym.

World events, though, didn't feature in my family; nothing was commented on, despite the daily arrival of newspapers and magazines. Things weren't noticed, or thought important enough, or had anything to do with us. So I don't know how I came to remember the Rosenbergs' trial in 1951, when I was eight. Julius and Ethel Rosenberg were tried and found guilty of espionage by a grand jury. They were condemned to die in the electric chair. In the years and months leading up to the hour of their death, there were many pleas for their lives to be saved. (In these days of Gorbachev *perestroika*, it is hard to envisage how great was the fear and hatred of the Russian peril in the USA.) Each day the chilling faces of the two Rosenbergs would stare out at us from the newspaper as a new plea was registered. I've no doubt that their pictures were intended to foster in us a fear of them, and what they represented. But it was the ineffable sadness of their faces that I recall – and the faces of their two young sons, who would be orphaned if their parents were put to death.

They did die, and McCarthy's America revelled in their cleansing of the world for their children's futures. Yet in an entirely inarticulate way I was shocked that people would be killed for such a 'crime', and secretly I knew that my family would not have agreed with me. Like my family and their society, I was hugely conservative, but notions of justice, freedom, and different political beliefs were given a terrible jolt in my early teenage years by the fate of the Rosenbergs.

I lived my teens in two modes – one public: confident, garrulous, busy, a 'high achiever'; the other private: anxious, silent, full of dread and consequent misery. My parents were by now manifestly unhappy with each other; they didn't argue in front of us, but neither did they talk to each other. And despite announcing to us one evening that they intended to separate, they stayed together for three or four more years – and in all those years, not a word was spoken by any of us as to when they would separate and what that would mean for us children. (Divorce was another taboo at that time, a shameful impossibility.) My sister and brother and I never whispered so much as a word about it; to this day I don't know what they thought or felt and I wish almost as much as anything that we'd been able to find the words to reach out to each other, but we couldn't. Today I can only guess that in staying so silent we hoped to ward off the possibility of their parting.

My emotional life was running riot in other directions too:

boys and kissing, breasts and being 'felt up' were terrifically on my mind and I enjoyed and agonised my way through many a guilty pleasure.

But girls and women were in my imagination and heart and refused all my attempts to dislodge them. I knew something about idolising, and having crushes at my all-girls school was tolerated if you were able to be self-mocking about it/her. Yet I was worried silly because my passions seemed so intense – and unthinkable – for two friends, and two older women. (Not for all four at the same time: I was too prissy for such extravagance, and loved each in turn.) I can see now that what I did to try and make these feelings acceptable to myself was to employ the medieval notion of 'courtly love' in regards to these love objects. In that way the bodily, carnal, lustful could be given no place. I could worship – and yearn – from the distance of never uttering such love. During these years I think I heard the word 'lesbian' spoken once and was seized with mortification, sure that something in my face was probably giving me away.

So my days felt literally split between being outwardly just an ordinary teenager, smooching in the dark at school dances until you were tapped on the shoulder by a reproving teacher, going to school football games with my friends to cheer on the boys (*de rigueur* dress was camelhair coats, loafers and a wool scarf), talking endlessly about whether Tom, Dick or Harry was the cutest.

Yet inwardly the hoping, endlessly hoping – for what? Something that couldn't exist, some gesture of intimacy from *her* that would involve neither word nor deed, an impossible desire of wanting and refusing to want at the same time. And as a further tortuous refinement of this, each of the girls and women I loved was Olympianly unobtainable, unequivocally heterosexual and unaware that I had feelings for them other than the 'innocent' ones of friendship.

Thirteen, fourteen, fifteen – each year felt weightier as my feelings became too insistent to ignore. I wasn't doing very well at keeping up the 'happy het' performance, but neither was I able to give voice to these other feelings.

My parents finally separated and we moved house with my mother, just out of reach of all my friends. So I lay on my bed at weekends and read. This was a pleasure (and an escape) that my mother and I shared. We didn't talk much about the novels we'd both read, but she'd pass on to me books and authors whom she'd enjoyed. One day she gave me a novel called *The Well of Loneliness* by Radclyffe Hall. Looking back, I try to remember whether she made any remark about it: I swear not. So I began it and was thunderstruck to find myself reading about a love affair between two women, Stephen Gordon and Mary Llewellyn. I hated it and I was transfixed. I read it clandestinely despite the fact that it had been given to me. (Interestingly, years later, in a particularly difficult conversation with my mother about my sexuality, she couldn't remember giving me the book at all.) I was appalled by it, and I've never looked at it again until now. What I remember loathing was Stephen's terrible self-hatred and her consequent coldness and cruelty to her lover. I had a sense too of despising Stephen's mannishness. But my feelings, I suspect, were confused about this as I too had absorbed society's fear and loathing of homosexuality, and its stereotyped notions that what all lesbians really wanted to be was a man and literally to pounce on all women. So the world of Stephen Gordon *et al* seemed a bleak and lonely one, and I became convinced that this was what I was condemned to.

I have less than a paragraph to write about the book, yet it kept its grip on me for many years. Later, how I envied the lucky young women of the 1970s whose first written account of lesbianism was the raunchy, assured, pleasure-seeking *Rubyfruit Jungle* by Rita Mae Brown. But at fifteen I hadn't learnt how to say to myself: Stephen is Radclyffe Hall's creation and there are as many ways to characterise lesbianism as there are heterosexuality. After all, Heathcliff and Cathy have no more in common with JR and Sue Ellen than Stephen and Mary have with the women lovers in June Arnold's engaging *Sister Gin*. But as I've said, I hadn't the knowledge to bring these questions to bear on *The Well of Loneliness*. I took it absolutely at face value and it spelt a desolation that I lived with for much too long.

But the early 1970s gave me the chance of a third transforming moment. I had moved to London after university and I was finding my feet in the film world, just on the edges of the counter-culture. What I did discover in those heady times was feminism, with its exhilarating vision of making the world anew. And it felt like that – the women's liberation movement was about us, for us, made by us, belonged to us, and that sense of 'us' was of all women. Nowadays, living with the cruel and limiting consequences of Thatcherism, that visionary sense can seem naive, but at the time it produced an optimism that fuelled us with enormous determination and confidence. We could undo all the constrictions and bonds that had held us, and for me that also meant no longer pretending to be what didn't bring me happiness – indeed, for years had made me feel unreal. I fell in love with a woman and she with me, and it was like a world transformed.

# CHARLOTTE GREIG

## *The Jimi Hendrix Experience*

I *am a musician and writer living in London. As this story tells,
much of my childhood was spent in a boarding school on the Kent
coast, where I was very happy. At the age of fourteen, I was
transferred to a school I hated. From then on I seemed to be in a
state of permanent rebellion, which lasted from adolescence right
through my twenties. Not until I was thirty did I find my niche. I
decided to enter a rap competition with a friend of mine, Sue
Thompson; we adopted the names Sue T and Lottie G, and much
to our amazement we won. This was no big deal in reality, but we
were ecstatic about our success and it gave us the push to go out and
perform. Female Force – as we called our crew – became the focal
point for our ambitions, and through performing I gained a new
confidence and a passion for music. I then began working at music
in earnest, both as a historian (in 1988 and '89 I wrote a book on
girl groups called* Will You Still Love Me Tomorrow?) *and as a
songwriter.*

I first saw the Jimi Hendrix Experience on 'Top of the Pops' in
1967, when I was thirteen years old. Jimi was in black and
white, in close-up; as for the Experience, like most people I
can't remember a thing about them. There were thirty or more
of us little girls sitting round the television set in the dark,
ranged in rows as though at the cinema, watching in horror and
fascination as Jimi brought us tidings from the outside world of
sex and drugs and rock and roll. Total silence reigned. The
heckling, jeering, cheering, poking and fighting that normally
accompanied our 'Top of the Pops' sessions suddenly stopped.
Jimi stood there like a bad dream come true: all Black, all

candyfloss hair, all scarves and beads and frills, with a look of calm defiance on his sallow face with its mangy half-beard. Quietly he unleashed chaos on our world as he began to torture his guitar right there in front of us, making it wail and writhe and howl. We watched wide-eyed until this gruesome perform-ance, for which we could find no explanation, ended; and then as the lights went up we returned, relieved, to our usual occupation of making bitchy comments about the dancers in the studio audience. We ignored what we had seen, but we did not forget it.

Next day – and it took us until next day to talk about it – we all agreed that Jimi Hendrix was the most repulsive man alive. Personally, I never liked him, even when I grew up. I could never quite forgive him for the shock he had given me, for intruding into 'Top of the Pops' in that way. Yet from that time on, in the back of my mind was the hope that something like the Jimi Hendrix Experience would happen again on 'Top of the Pops' – something extraordinary, frightening and real. It never did, but twenty years later I still watch the programme every week, vainly expecting some monstrous demon to burst into the studio and scare the wits out of everyone.

It was a long time before I realised that seeing Jimi Hendrix on television had been a transforming moment in my life, a sign that something unspeakable existed beneath – or was it above – the marooned little world I knew and loved as a child.

During the sixties I and my twin sister were living in a boarding school on the coast of Kent. To begin with we had missed home desperately and had spent the first few weeks of our first term shivering miserably in the bitter cold winds that blew off the sea there, wearing the wrong school uniforms and sticking out like a couple of sore red thumbs. At night the girls in the dormitories told us stories to scare us about sex maniacs who came out at night on the fire escapes and rattled the windows. I didn't know exactly what sex maniacs were but they sounded terrifying, and I lay awake listening to the windows rattle and dreading their appearance. But nothing terrible ever happened; after a few months I stopped being scared, and the gloom of those wretched, abandoned winter days lifted.

As it turned out, the school was a perfect place to grow up in. It was a big old place by the sea on the Isle of Thanet, right by the North Foreland lighthouse. Every night we lay in bed and watched its beams, counting the seconds in between each shaft of light, until we fell asleep. There were long winters when the foghorn that had frightened us at first began to sound familiar, booming reassuringly all day long; and summers when we swam after supper and played outside until dark. I began to feel pleasantly cut off from the world on my own little island in the sea. The nuns and lay teachers who ran the school brought us up in an atmosphere of benevolent, absent-minded liberalism. To them, we were all blessed; we could do no real wrong.

As far as the nuns were concerned, the likes of Jimi Hendrix held no threat of evil over us; to them he seemed no more than a childish fantasy, a bogeyman dreamed up by silly adolescent girls to frighten themselves. We were protected by their love, by God's love – so they thought. I took comfort from the nuns' indulgent smiles as we told them what we had seen on television, but somehow I could never quite, like them, relegate Jimi to the cast of childhood demons who in the landscape of our imagin-ation surrounded the safety of our school: the sex maniacs on the fire escape, the dog that came out to get you if you played on the bottom games field for too long on a summer evening, the mad old woman who lived on the beach in winter, inside the rusty tea house with the swinging doors. The presence of these evil spirits had been felt, never seen; but Jimi was different: for a start, he was real. Jimi had walked into the world of the nice, stupid people who danced on 'Top of the Pops' and got on to television, which had beamed him right through the magic, charmed circle the nuns had drawn round our school. He had stood before us, the Devil incarnate. Then he had performed ritual murder on his guitar, and no one had stopped him. His performance had electrified us, glued to the screen in the dark; but the nuns had remained impassive, refusing to admit defeat, refusing to acknowledge what had happened; so, it seemed to me, either they were blind or they were lying.

At that time, Jimi Hendrix was the only blot on my landscape, the only intimation of danger, the one distant threat to my happy, secure existence under the lighthouse. It was not that the nuns tried to maintain our childish innocence by keeping us locked away from the world – far from it; but they made us feel safe from any harm, safe from the Jimis of this world.

By the age of fourteen, we were having a lot of fun at school. Saturday was the best day of the week. In the morning we would go into town and buy sweets and tights, or steal Evette make-up from Woolworth's. I was always too scared to do it, but I stood guard for my friends and was sometimes rewarded by a pale pink lipstick or a sea-green eyeshadow. In the afternoons we watched the Monkees on television – they, thank God, were light years away from the dreaded Jimi Hendrix. The show always began and ended, as I remember, with the boys on go-carts, singing:

> Hey hey we're the Monkees,
> People say we monkey around,
> But we're too busy singing
> To put anybody down.

We loved the Monkees because they were chummy boys, and that was the only sort of boys we liked. Nobody could really fancy one of the Monkees, we felt; Mike Nesmith had that silly woolly hat, Micky Dolenz's grin was a little too like a real monkey's, Davy Jones was too short and too English, and Peter Tork's possible attractions could not even be so much as contemplated on account of his awful pudding-basin haircut. But these shortcomings were what made us feel secure; and like the Monkees, we were too busy swinging along in the pop world to put anybody down. We knew that with the Monkees, we were safe from anything nasty like Jimi Hendrix rearing his ugly head. And that was exactly how we wanted it to be.

It was the same with our parties. These were held once a month or so on a Saturday or Sunday evening in the school gym. All the older girls in the school were invited, and our main interest was to watch each other dance and learn all the different steps and styles. We had a stock of four records, which all belonged to a girl named Vicky Hamilton from Maidstone, who had two very fashionable older brothers. (I had seen them once when they came to open day wearing sunglasses and Chelsea boots.) Our favourite one was 'Good Vibrations' by the Beach Boys; it wasn't much good for dancing to, but we loved it because the voices were high, like girls', and the whole thing sounded beautiful and religious and psychedelic, like early-morning chapel with the nuns singing chants and Father O'Brien waving the golden incense holder back and forth and Sister Gladioli going mad on the organ. Next best was 'Think' by Aretha Franklin, with its warning, 'You better think – Think! – what you're trying to do to me!' and its crescendo of 'Freedom, freedom, freedom, whoah freedom!', rousing words that meant nothing to us but sounded fantastically exciting. We also had two other good dance records: the Rolling Stones' 'Get Off My Cloud' and Brenton Wood's 'Gimme Little Sign':

> Just gimme some kind of sign, girl
> Oh my baby
> To show me that you're mine girl, all right.

Brenton Wood, whom we had seen on television, was a minority interest in our school, but he was my hero. He was slick and suave, cool and sophisticated, and not in the least like the vile Jimi Hendrix. I was the only girl in my form who really cared about Brenton, so it seemed that he was singing to me alone when he fixed me with his brown eyes and pleaded 'Just gimme some kind of sign, girl'. Would I do such a thing, I wondered?

Could I? What did it mean, 'some kind of sign'? I just couldn't decide.

Such gentle reflections abruptly ceased when my sister and I left our boarding school in Kent and were sent to another in Gloucestershire, which I hated with a passion. From the first moment I arrived there, it seemed to me that my life had gone completely wrong. I hated everyone and everything. I dropped my interest in music altogether and started writing long diaries, imagining myself as some pale young Romantic surrounded by philistines. My new teachers were mainly unpleasant and vindictive, or so I thought; they did nothing but watch us, lie in wait for us, and then pounce with some accusation or other. They were as different from the benevolent, placid nuns as could be. For them, the likes of Jimi Hendrix were all too real; sex-maniac bogeymen lurked in every dark corner of every coffee bar and depraved young girls made secret trysts with them whenever they had a chance. Perhaps the old bags were right; we girls had by now grown up, and we knew that sooner or later one of us would 'do it', as we called having sex. 'Have you done it?' we would ask each other after the summer holidays, and we would gather together at night to pool our information and glean a few tips should the occasion arise in the near future. But none of us could ever report anything more than quick goodbyes at parties, fumbled gropings into our jumpers, or slimy tongues darting between our clenched teeth.

Such brief encounters held no mystery for us, but were treated as a huge joke; on the whole, we suffered some hapless boy's amorous advances only so that we could give our friends a blow-by-blow account later and have them double up with laughter. So what was all the fuss about? There was obviously more to sex than gropings from the spotty boys of the Cirencester Agricultural College, or our teachers wouldn't have been so hysterical about it. Some evil power must lurk there.

My mind went back to Jimi Hendrix, because he was the only person I could think of who possibly had something to do with all this. Something had stirred in me, in all of us, that time we saw him on television at school in Kent, when he had scared and revolted us so much. Surely that feeling could not be sex? The nuns had smiled indulgently at Jimi; the teachers at my new school were afraid of him. What could I make of their reactions? Was Jimi real? Was danger real? Did it become real if you feared it? Or was it all something to do with growing up? I couldn't get to the bottom of it.

Then I began to understand that seeing Jimi Hendrix on television had, for me, marked the point when I grew up. At thirteen I had realised, not that the neat picture of good and evil painted for me by adults was a sham, but that I had outgrown it. Perhaps, I reflected at sixteen, the nuns had known that all along, and that was why they remained so unperturbed. Or maybe they were as naive as they seemed. Perhaps they knew less about Jimi Hendrix than me, perhaps more. Either way, they hadn't let on. I was going to have to find out for myself.

# PRISCILLA PRESLEY

## *Loving You*

Priscilla Beaulieu's father was in the United States Air Force, so her childhood was spent moving from one posting to another. When she was fourteen the family was sent to Wiesbaden in West Germany. Elvis Presley, then the idol of teenagers both sides of the Atlantic, was serving in nearby Bad Neuheim.

They met and began a fourteen-year love affair, with Elvis as her mentor. He tried to mould her into his perfect woman, dictating everything about her appearance. She left him, taking their daughter Lisa Marie with her, to try and pursue life on her own terms, but they remained close friends until his death. She is now an actress, playing Jenna in the television series 'Dallas'. She has written a book, Elvis and Me, about her time with Elvis.

There was a place called the Eagles Club, where American service families went for dinner and entertainment. Every day after school, I'd go to the snack bar there and listen to the jukebox and write letters to my friends back home, telling them how much I missed them.

One warm summer afternoon, I was sitting with my brother Don when I noticed a handsome man in his twenties staring at me. I'd seen him watching me before, but I'd never paid any attention to him. This time, he stood up and walked towards me. He introduced himself as Currie Grant and asked my name.

'Priscilla Beaulieu,' I said, immediately suspicious; he was much older than I.

He asked where in the States I came from, how I liked Germany, and if I liked Elvis Presley.

'Of course,' I said, laughing. 'Who doesn't?'

'I'm a good friend of his. My wife and I go to his house quite often. How would you like to join us one evening?'

Unprepared for such an extraordinary invitation, I grew even more skeptical and guarded. I told him I'd have to ask my parents. Over the course of the next two weeks, Currie met my parents and my father checked out his credentials. Currie assured Dad that I'd be well chaperoned when we visited Elvis, who lived off-base in a house in Bad Neuheim.

On the appointed night I tore through my closet, trying to find an appropriate outfit. Nothing seemed dressy enough for meeting Elvis Presley. I settled on a navy and white sailor dress and white socks and shoes. Surveying myself in the mirror, I thought I looked cute, but being only fourteen, I didn't think I'd make any kind of impression on Elvis.

Currie pulled up to an ordinary-looking three-story house surrounded by a white picket fence.

There was a sign on the gate in German, which translated as: AUTOGRAPHS BETWEEN 7.00 AND 8.00 P.M. ONLY. Even though it was after eight o'clock, a large group of friendly German girls waited around expectantly. When I asked Currie about them, he explained that there were always large groups of fans outside the house.

The plain, almost drab living room was filled with people, but I spotted Elvis immediately. He was handsomer than he appeared in films, younger and more vulnerable-looking with his GI haircut. He was in civilian clothes, a bright red sweater and tan slacks, and he was sitting with one leg swung over the arm of a large overstuffed chair, with a cigar dangling from his lips.

As Currie led me over to him, Elvis stood up and smiled. 'Well,' he said. 'What have we here?'

I didn't say anything. I couldn't. I just kept staring at him.

'Elvis,' Currie said, 'this is Priscilla Beaulieu. The girl I told you about.'

We shook hands and he said, 'Hi, I'm Elvis Presley,' but then there was a silence between us until Elvis asked me to sit down beside him, and Currie drifted off.

'So,' Elvis said. 'Do you go to school?'

'Yes.'

'What are you, about a junior or senior in high school?'

I blushed and said nothing, not willing to reveal that I was only in the ninth grade.

'Well,' he persisted.'

'Ninth.'

Elvis looked confused. 'Ninth what?'

'Grade,' I whispered.

'Ninth *grade*,' he said, and started laughing. 'Why, you're just a baby.'

'Thanks,' I said curtly. Not even Elvis Presley had the right to say that to me.

'Well. Seems the little girl has spunk,' he said, laughing again, amused by my response. He gave me that charming smile of his, and all my resentment just melted away.

We made small talk for a while longer. Then Elvis got up and walked over to the piano and sat down. The room suddenly grew silent. Everyone's eyes were riveted on him as he began to entertain us.

I was nervous. I glanced around the room and saw an intimidating life-size poster of a half-nude Brigitte Bardot on the wall. She was the last person I wanted to see, with her fulsome body, pouting lips, and wild mane of tousled hair. Imagining Elvis's taste in women, I felt very young and out of place.

I glanced up and saw Elvis trying to get my attention. I noticed that the less response I showed, the more he began singing just for me. I couldn't believe that Elvis Presley was trying to impress me.

Later he asked me to come into the kitchen, where he introduced me to his grandmother, Minnie Mae Presley, who stood by the stove, frying a huge pan of bacon. As we sat down at the table, I told Elvis I wasn't hungry. Actually I was too nervous to eat.

'You're the first girl I've met from the States in a long time,' Elvis said, as he began devouring the first of five gigantic bacon sandwiches, each one smothered with mustard. 'Who are the kids listening to?'

I laughed. 'Are you kidding?' I said. 'Everyone listens to you.'

It felt like we'd just begun talking when Currie came in and pointed to his watch. I had dreaded that moment; the evening had gone so fast. It seemed I had just arrived, and now I was being hurried away. Elvis and I had just started to get to know each other. I felt like Cinderella, knowing that when my curfew came, all this magic would end. I was surprised when Elvis asked Currie if I could possibly stay longer. When Currie explained the agreement with my father, Elvis casually suggested that maybe I could come by again. Though I wanted to more than anything in the world, I didn't really believe it would happen.

The fog was so thick on the Autobahn back to Wiesbaden that I didn't get home until 2 a.m. My parents had waited up, wanting to know everything that had happened. I told them Elvis was a gentleman, that he was funny and entertained his friends all night, and that I'd had a wonderful time.

The next day in school, I couldn't concentrate. My thoughts were entirely on Elvis. I tried to recall every word he'd said to me, every song he'd sung, every look in his eyes as he'd gazed at me. I went over and over our conversation. His charm was captivating. I told no one. Who would ever believe that just the night before, I'd been with Elvis Presley?

I never expected to hear from him again. Then, a few days later, the phone rang. It was Currie. He said he'd just got a call from Elvis, who wondered if it was possible for Currie to bring me over that night. I was ecstatic.

The next visit was very much like the one before – small talk, singing, Elvis playing the piano, and everyone eating Grandma's favorite dishes. But later, when Elvis had finished singing, he came up to me. 'I want to be alone with you, Priscilla.'

We were standing face to face, staring into each other's eyes. I looked around. The room was empty.

'We are alone,' I replied nervously.

He moved closer, backing me against the wall. 'I mean *really* alone,' he whispered. 'Will you come upstairs to my room?'

The question threw me into a panic. *His room?*

Until that moment, it hadn't crossed my mind that Elvis Presley might be interested in me sexually. He could have any girl in the world. Why would he want me?

'There's nothing to be frightened of, honey.'

As he spoke, he was smoothing my hair. 'I swear I'll never do anything to harm you.' He sounded absolutely sincere. 'I'll treat you just like a sister.' Flustered and confused, I looked away.

'Please.'

Standing there looking into his eyes, I was drawn to him almost against my will. I believed him; it wasn't a difficult thing to do. I had discovered by now his intentions were warm and sincere. Moments went by and I still couldn't do anything. Then I nodded. 'All right, I'll go.'

He took my hand and led me toward the stairs, whispering which room was his, and said, 'You go on ahead, and I'll join you in a few minutes. It looks better.'

He headed toward the kitchen as I slowly climbed the stairs, wondering, What would he demand of me? Expect of me? I will be completely alone with him for the first time. Since meeting him I had dreamed of this moment, sure that it would never arrive, and now I was in the midst of a reality I'd never expected.

I reached the second floor and found his bedroom. I went in and sat down primly on a stiff-backed chair – and waited. When Elvis didn't show up after a few minutes, I began to look around. It was an ordinary room with nothing unusual, certainly nothing to imply that it belonged to a famous rock-and-roll singer. There were several letters from girls in the States on his night table. I wanted to read the letters but was afraid he'd catch me.

It was another twenty minutes before he finally appeared. He came in, removed his jacket, turned on the radio, and then sat down on his bed. I hardly looked at him, petrified of what he might expect. I imagined him grabbing me, throwing me down on the bed, and making love to me.

Instead he said, 'Why don't you come over here and sit next to me?' I was reluctant, but he assured me that I had nothing to be afraid of. 'I really like you, Priscilla. You're refreshing. It's nice to talk to someone from back home. I miss that. It gets a little lonely here.'

I sat next to him, saying nothing, but I was touched by his vulnerable, boyish quality. He went on to say that our relationship was going to be important to him and that he needed me. It was October and he was scheduled to return to the States in six months. He knew lots of girls, he said, and many had come to visit as I had, but I was the first girl with whom he felt a real closeness.

I cuddled into his arms, certain he would not move too fast. He held me closely.

My heart went out to Elvis that night as he confided his problems and worries. He was a world-famous entertainer, a great star, and yet a terribly lonely man.

Again our visit seemed to end too soon. He kissed me goodbye, my first real kiss. I had never experienced such a mixture of affection and desire. I was speechless but closely tied to the reality of where I was – locked in his arms, my mouth against his. Aware of my response – and my youth – he broke away first, saying, 'We have plenty of time, little one.' He kissed my forehead and sent me home.

By our fourth date, Dad had laid down the law. 'If you want

to continue seeing Elvis, we're going to have to meet him.' My parents weren't so enthralled with his celebrity status that they were willing to compromise their principles. One Saturday night I said to Elvis, 'My parents want to meet you. They want you to pick me up.'

He bristled. 'What do you mean?'

'I mean,' I said nervously, 'I can't come see you any more unless you come and meet my parents.'

He agreed – provided he could bring his father along.

That day I went through my usual routine except instead of being ready one hour in advance it was two. I waited by the window, looking for his car as I played his records nonstop until my father yelled from the kitchen, 'Do you have to play those records now? My God, the man will be here in a few minutes and you see him practically every night. I'd think you'd want to take a breather from each other.'

About an hour later, I spotted Elvis's BMW and saw Elvis and his father emerge from the car. Elvis had come totally prepared; he was wearing his uniform to impress Dad. He knew that the service was their connection, and he played on it. He looked great.

He took off his hat and kissed me on the cheek. I asked him and his father in and led them into our living room, where Elvis fidgeted and seemed, for once, at a loss for words. 'Are your parents here?' he ventured. I could manage only a nod, and he continued, 'I know we're a little late, but I had to get cleaned up – and we had some trouble finding the place.'

Instead of saying 'Hi', as most young men would have done, Elvis put out his hand and said, 'Hello, I'm Elvis Presley and this is my daddy, Vernon.'

It sounded silly to me; they knew who he was, as did the whole world. But Elvis was the perfect gentleman. My father was visibly impressed, and from that moment on, Elvis always addressed him as Captain Beaulieu or Sir.

I sat attentively, observing Elvis's uneasiness and remembering his relaxed manner in his own home. He was on his best behavior, and it was endearing. Mother was reserving judgement about this rock-and-roll star she had professed to dislike so much. I could see that his Southern charm was winning her over.

Finally, my father got around to explaining to Elvis the Beaulieu dating rules. If he wanted to see me, Elvis had to pick me up and bring me home. Elvis explained that by the time he got off duty, went home, cleaned up, came to Wiesbaden and back, the evening would be gone. Would it be all right if his father would collect me?

Dad mulled this over, then expressed his concern. 'Just what is the intent here? Let's face it: you're Elvis Presley. You have women throwing themselves at you. Why my daughter?'

Elvis said, 'Well, Sir, I happen to be very fond of her. She's a lot more mature than her age and I enjoy her company. It hasn't been easy for me, being away from home and all. It gets kinda lonely. I guess you might say I need someone to talk to. You don't have to worry about her, Captain. I'll take good care of her.'

Elvis's honesty disarmed Dad, just as it did my mother. I joined Elvis as he stood, picked up his hat, and added, 'Well, Sir, we've got a long drive.'

There was one stipulation: Elvis himself had to bring me home. He agreed, reassuring them that I would be well taken care of, that there were a lot of family members at his house. He could have ridiculed Dad's request, yet he agreed to take me home every night. I was thrilled but contained my excitement. He *really* wanted to be with me.

*This extract is from* Elvis and Me, *(Century Hutchinson, 1985)*

# ANNE KARPF

....................................

## *The Italian Lesson*

I *was born in London in 1950, the daughter of Polish Jews who
were survivors of the Holocaust and came to England after the
Second World War. I went to a very academic direct grant school
in London and then spent three fairly unhappy years at St Hilda's
College, Oxford, (occasionally) studying philosophy, politics and
economics, and then English language and literature. My first job
after graduating was BBC television researcher, but I left in 1976
after I couldn't bear to make another flabby liberal social problem
documentary. Since then I've been a freelance journalist and critic,
contributing regularly to the* Guardian, *the* Observer, *and* The
Listener. *I'm also a contributing editor to* Cosmopolitan, *and I do
some radio and television broadcasting, though I prefer to hide
away in my back room and write. In 1981 I completed, by part-
time study, an MSc. in the sociology of health and illness, and have
taught medical sociology. My first book,* Doctoring the Media:
The Reporting of Health and Medicine, *was published in 1988,
and I'm currently writing a book on my parents' experiences during
the war, and my own as a child of survivors.*

....................................

You could call it my chrysalis period, my stay in Florence when
I was eighteen. It helped me to mutate from a caterpillar into
some kind of butterfly. It took me away from home.

The days leading up to it were charged with terror. Perhaps
it hadn't been such a good idea, after all, to spend three months
between school and university studying history of art and Italian
at the University of Florence. My friends had no problem
hitching hither and travelling thither, but I did, and when I

boldly conceived this plan and persuaded two of them to join me, for once I failed to take into account my extreme nervousness about being away from home and family.

The plan had originated in a family holiday two years earlier, when I visited Florence for the first time: inhaling the city and buoyant with its colour and energy, I'd blithely announced, 'I'm going to come and study here'. Now I wasn't so sure.

My previous solo trips abroad had been eventful. My parents' first attempt to prise me away from home – a Swiss finishing-school summer holiday – I refused altogether. Too scary – and I didn't want to miss 'Emergency Ward 10' on television. (My sister went alone, and got expelled for jumping out of a first-floor window for a midnight assignation with a boy from a neighbouring school. She seemed to have both her own share of pluck and mine.) Their second try got me fixed up with an exchange visit to the South of France. Aged fifteen, clutching my new passport, I missed the train at Calais and in schoolgirl French had to find a hotel to stay overnight. In Paris the next day the train was full, but I tearfully contrived to get picked up by a French count who showed me Paris by night, and dined me in an expensive Left Bank restaurant. It made a good story, but it didn't persuade my parents or me that I was a competent traveller, and to avoid further mishap, they insisted that my return journey should be by plane.

On my third solo venture abroad, I fetched up with the same exchange French schoolgirl, who took advantage of her parents' absence to live it up with a group of Parisians who all ignored me. I spent the first few days crying into my pillow, and the rest gasping in terror on the back of a callow youth's motorbike as he careered recklessly round the Arc de Triomphe.

If all this sounds amusing, it wasn't. I was an anxious, insecure girl, sustained only by academic success and a nervous attachment to my parents. As a teenager, my place seemed always on the outside, looking in: on the fringe of a group, I would tag on tenuously, trailing after the belongers and leaders.

And this was the 1960s when, according to the prevailing wisdom, everyone was loose and hanging free – everyone but me. I spent the 1960s tightly coiled and rigid. Boyfriends seemed wholly unattainable: there was no way I could survive the intimacy. So I made do with fantasy lovers and a richly imagined socal life.

The train which pulled out of Waterloo took me not only to another country but to a different world. It sped me from my family and the shadow of my good-looking, bubbly older sister, against whom I could never measure up. Now, for the first time, I had no one to compare myself to; I could make it up myself. And if I made it up in her image, at least it was still mine.

In Florence, I embraced life where before I'd shrunk from it. After years as a diffident follower, I became an initiator. We were three students at the university, and as the most fluent Italian speaker in our group and the one who looked most like a native, I was the bridge between us and them. What's more, when I got chatted up by an architecture student working in the university canteen (he gave me a free plate of chips as an emblem of his affection) and consented to a date, a whole network of social contacts panned out. And it fell to me to introduce my friends to these new mates.

On Italian holidays, my sister had mooned over Italian boyfriends and crooned Italian pop hits. Now I had both of my own in profusion. 'Ma che freddo fa', 'La notte' – I can sing them still, and they evoke more powerful emotions than words can describe: the intensity of feeling known, liked, desired, and free for the first time.

I sometimes think I must have been Italian in a previous life. In Florence, the shy, self-conscious me who hovered outside made way for a dominant, impulsive person who entered and acted. I picked up local argot and inflections, and people often mistook me for an Italian. I was more expansive than I'd ever been in public before, though I also had my first (conscious) taste of depression. I acquired a gleaming set of social skills. I learned to chat to people I didn't know, to ask the loosening question, to elicit the flowing answer. I discovered how to give the impression of being deep. (This was an enduring preoccupation of my teenage years and twenties, I recall.) And I fell for someone.

I'd noticed Sakis in my first week. He was beautiful, with a fine mouth, high cheekbones, soft dark hair, and manly looks. (Under my adoring gaze his somewhat short stature and naff, transparent fitted black shirts evaporated.) I tried everything to get him to notice me, but without success. So I gave up. I had one boyfriend (an achievement in itself), and another. And then, one week before I was to leave, we met. It turned out that he'd never even noticed me before (so much for all my efforts). He was Greek, and an architecture student, and he fell for me too. For the first time, and with the security of my imminent departure, I opened the door to intimacy.

For a week we had a passionate relationship, conducted to the sounds of a Greek pop group, 'Aphrodite's Child' (among its members, I reluctantly recall, one Demis Roussos) and an Italian pop song, 'La Bambola' (a parting gift which became to me something of a religious relic). And we ate nocturnal (3 a.m.) pizzas in a famous pizza restaurant where the transvestite strippers would come to eat after their shows.

Holiday romances are easily mocked, but for me it was the first time ever that I'd set out to attract and (eventually) succeeded. I felt exhilarated. And my taste was good: naff he may have been, and no intellectual either, but Sakis was kind and adoring, continuing to send me love letters for years after.

Florence opened me up in other ways, too. I loved walking the streets on my own. At school I'd been a virtuous pupil, dutiful in behaviour and school work, swotting strenuously for exams. In Florence, I became a bad pupil. I skipped classes, didn't buy the books. By the end, I was attending no lessons at all. I swapped formal schooling entirely for informal learning. I visited a different museum, gallery, or painting each day, and made them my own. I took in their qualities in a wholly unacademic way. I had no theoretical or historical knowledge of art and I never acquired it, but I learned to relish and become excited by my own private experience of painting and sculpture.

The detail of the city thrilled me too. A routine journey to the shops might offer a glimpsed wrought-iron gate or jewel of a courtyard. The Campanile, Giotto's pink and white gateau-like bell-tower, I could see from my bed without stirring when I awoke. It sounds like the stuff of women's magazines, but it was true: for the first time ever I risked enthusiasm – over food, painting, markets, men.

Leaving was terrible, like the forcible extraction of a tooth. It felt as if I was leaving part of myself, the new part, behind. Back in London, I was achingly depressed for the summer, until my first term at university offered its own absorbing panics.

Florence was the beginning of my adult self. It gave me a glimmering of myself as an independent, sociable and lovable person. It also taught me social skills which I was to milk to the full in my subsequent (and unhappy) years as a student.

Ironically, I learned those skills too well. The me that emerged in Florence – confident and popular – came to mask all the others – the diffident, tentative, and shy self which I have latterly and painfully come to excavate and respect. The Florence me was only a temporary and partial me, one I've had in some sense to unlearn. But in Florence, I got my first whiff of joy.

# DIANE ABBOTT

......................................................

## *Young, Gifted and Black*

I was born in London at St Mary's Hospital, Harrow Road, Paddington, on the 27th of September 1953. My parents were Jamaican immigrants. My father was a sheet-metal worker who died some years ago. My mother is a retired health service worker. I was educated at Harrow County Grammar School for Girls and Newnham College, Cambridge.

I have worked as an administrative trainee with the Home Office, race relations officer with the National Council for Civil Liberties and a journalist with Thames Television and TV AM. I've also worked in public relations. From 1982 to 1986 I was a councillor on Westminster City Council. I was elected to Parliament in 1987.

......................................................

I vividly remember the day I made up my mind to go to Cambridge University. It was summer, a school outing, and we went there by coach. Normally school outings were more about the sandwiches and the novelty than the actual destination. But Cambridge captured my imagination. There was the river, the medieval lanes and spires and the green lawns. And my naive, adolescent eye was enchanted by the students. There were crowds of them, sauntering around in the sunshine in striped scarves. They seemed happy, confident and masters of all they surveyed. It was all a world away from the London suburb where I grew up. I made up my mind that this was heaven, they were gods and that I would go there. And I was to hold unswervingly to this ambition in the years to come.

I had the confidence that only unbounded ignorance can give. I had no idea what a leap it represented in class terms. In truth

I had only a dim idea of how the British class system worked. To grow up Black in Britain is to grow up an outsider, and in any case, this was the sixties with its cult of egalitarianism. My main source of information on current affairs was the *Daily Mirror*, Hugh Cudlipp's exuberantly classless *Mirror*. So as far as I knew, the upper classes were a joke and everybody else was more or less equal. Sometimes, of course, things happened that I couldn't explain. For years my best friend in junior school was Margaret. She was quiet and soft-spoken and I have a vivid recollection of her big grey eyes. Every so often she would have a friend home to tea. But it was never me; always the same blonde girl whom neither of us liked and Margaret hardly spoke to at school. I never questioned why I was not an acceptable friend for Margaret to bring home; never even formulated it in my mind like that. There are so many inexplicable phenomena in a child's world; it was just one more. In the same way I did not appreciate why it should be particularly remarkable that a Black girl should go to Cambridge. I took no advice, confided in no one and, blissfully ignorant of the fact that it couldn't be done, went ahead and did it.

First I had to overcome what might best be described as the scepticism of my teachers. I had none of the virtues which endear children to teachers. I was rotten at games – this to the bafflement of my gym mistress, who used to say: 'But you West Indian girls are supposed to be good at netball.' I was always late, always losing things, perpetually disorganised, a natural loner, and I liked to challenge authority.

Only looking back do I realise what else about me irritated some teachers so much: I was the only Black girl in an all-white suburban grammar school. But there again not quite understanding the roots of the hostility was, curiously, a kind of protective shield. And, whatever their reason for disliking me, most infuriating of all must have been the fact that I was actually rather clever. From my long-suffering teachers' point of view it was bad enough that I was an invariable source of schoolgirl disaffection, a maelstrom of disorganisation and missing personal belongings. The fact that I calmly refused to attend English classes in the sixth form because I felt I wasn't learning anything, without considering that I was offering a mortal insult to my poor teacher, made matters worse. But that I also picked up ten O levels and four A levels (nearly all Grade As) was to my teachers sheer searing injustice. It was to take years for me to appreciate just how infuriating some people find achievement without apparent effort.

If I didn't understand just how out of the ordinary it would be for a working-class Black girl to go to Cambridge, my teachers certainly did. So when I raised the question of me sitting the Oxford and Cambridge entrance exam with them, I was met with a certain coolness. And I had to raise it. If I had waited for them to suggest it I would be serving in Woolworth's to this very day.

'I don't think,' my teacher said in a measured way, 'that you are really up to it.'

'But I do,' I said, 'and that's what matters, isn't it?'

It was one of the genuinely pivotal moments of my life.

When she realised I was set on the idea, my teacher obliquely raised the class issue. 'What daily paper do you read?' she said.

All innocence, I said: 'The *Daily Mirror*.'

She turned away, made a face, and from then on used to bring in old *Weekly Guardian*s for me to study.

To get into Cambridge at that time to read an arts subject you also had to take, and pass, a Latin exam. My Latin teacher told me briskly and irritably early on that I would certainly fail.

The other girl who took the Oxford and Cambridge exams was called Penny. She was the star pupil, and she was everything I was not: tall, slim, white, middle-class and quiet. Quiet to the point of being languid; far too languid to cause trouble. I have never heard of her since.

But in the face of my insistence my teachers agreed, with no great enthusiasm, to enter and tutor me for the Oxford and Cambridge entrance exams alongside the exemplary Penny.

Once I had squared my teachers, my family presented another set of problems. For one thing, Cambridge was way outside the limits of their aspirations for me. They were working-class Jamaicans who had immigrated to this country in the fifties. They wanted me to get an education and a good job, of course, but in their world a good job was any sort of office job or possibly a staff nurse. I had always been a slightly odd child, dreamy, impractical and always reading. In bed, in the bath, on family outings, at the dinner table, even walking down the steet to perform an errand, I would have my nose in a book. I read very fast, three books a day in the summer holidays, and I was completely omnivorous. At the age of eleven a dinner lady casually asked me what was my favourite book. I shyly told the astonished woman that it was H. H. Munroe's *Saki* and added, for good measure, that I thought 'she was a good cook as cooks go, but as cooks go she went' was the cleverest line in the English language. My bookishness was a byword in my family and my desire to go to Cambridge was just another one of my dimly understood eccentricities.

Then, just before my O levels, my mother left home. As well as all the psychological attendant dramas, there was an assumption that I would take on all her domestic duties. No one questioned it; not even me. I was a poor and uninterested housekeeper. I overstocked on some things so they went mouldy and ran out of others. My gravy was dreadful and only my brother really understood how to make the washing machine work. But housekeeper I was, at sixteen with ten O levels to sit and a father whose violent and uncertain temper made me dread going home. And my father never failed to remind me that at my age other girls (meaning other Black girls) were at work. He was perfectly correct, but in the circumstances I didn't discuss reading history at Cambridge with him, still less enlist his support.

It would have been easy at one stage to give up on the idea of Cambridge. My teachers weren't enthusiastic, my father was uncomprehending, my two best friends had left school to go to secretarial college and I was by then combining four A levels with my desultory efforts at housework. Home was a nightmare because of the inevitable tensions of my parents' divorce and my father's violence. I was desperate to leave, but doing the Oxbridge entrance meant an extra term at school and in effect a further year at home. And my boyfriend, the main source of support and affection in my life, went off to university at Bath, the other end of the country from my desired dreaming spires. No one I knew had gone to Oxbridge; no one I knew was going there. It took a will of iron to pursue the idea, but it never occurred to me to drop it.

I left home and went to stay with friends of the family in order to complete the extra term. My father was furious.

Finally, despite everything which had gone wrong and my parents' prophecies of doom, the day came when I had to sit the written exam. I remember on that day there was a particularly dramatic morning sky – pink and grey and banks of clouds. I took it as a sign that everything was going to be all right.

Then I had to travel to Cambridge for the interview. I don't know how it went but then, as now, I was fluent and I could talk. Curiously, although I wanted to go there so badly, I don't remember how it felt to get the news that I had got a place. There certainly wasn't mass rejoicing.

For one thing I was by now staying with my boyfriend's parents who, although they were nice to me for their son's sake, were so horrified by the thought of Black grandchildren that they couldn't quite bring themselves to celebrate my triumphs. My boyfriend was hundreds of miles away in Bath; my teachers thought I was undeserving; my father thought I was ungrateful and my mother, who was by now living in Huddersfield, had secretly hoped I would agree to go to Huddersfield Polytechnic.

But I hadn't done it for any of them, I had done it for myself; I was pleased, but had no sense of superhuman achievement.

I spent the time between school and Cambridge doing a succession of clerical jobs. My mother and my boyfriend's mother spent it amassing what they believed was a suitable wardrobe for a lady student. Neither of them had been to university, but they did their best. My mother scoured the markets of Huddersfield, where she lived, and put together a fine collection of acrylic jumpers and polyester twin-sets. My boyfriend's mother, a demon on the sewing machine, bought a job lot of green and brown Crimplene. From this she fashioned a series of outfits. There was a green Crimplene cape, green Crimplene suit, green Crimplene trousers, green Crimplene jerkin, and so on. And another whole set of outfits in brown. The combinations were presumably infinite and it was a carefully made set of clothes designed to last me a lifetime. To coordinate with it I had the jumpers my mother had bought me. They dutifully packed my bags and waved me off to Cambridge. This was the wardrobe to go to university in, and they were proud of themselves.

Years later a friend of mine who also read history told me he clearly remembers seeing me in the first week when the history people were gathered together. There I was all in green, and he reckoned he had never seen anyone look so naive in all his life. Within days I had realised that green Crimplene suits were not what the fashionable students wore, and by the end of term I had got together the orthodox set of denim and Indian printed cotton clothes.

I do remember my first day. All the history first years gathered in our tutor's study and we sat on the floor while she talked. I looked around me. Cambridge was my 'shining city' and I had done it; I had got there. I didn't then appreciate quite how big the odds were against me doing what I had done. But I knew I had overcome indifference, hostility and all the practical obstacles and, through sheer effort of will, achieved my heart's desire. But as I looked around, and before I could even begin to savour a sense of triumph, something slowly began to dawn. I had asked no one, taken no advice. On the contrary, the more I had met resistance, the more I had persisted. But my knowledge of Cambridge was limited to one coach trip one sunny afternoon years ago and what I had gleaned from novels. I took in my fellow students demurely sitting cross-legged on the floor. They all looked like clones of my erstwhile tutorial companion, Penny: nice, bland, white middle-class girls. For the first time the radiant and compelling vision of Cambridge on that summer afternoon so long ago began to dim. I realised I wasn't like them, could never be like them, and furthermore had no plans to become like them. I began to wonder if I hadn't made the biggest mistake of my life.

I was right and I was wrong. I was right to grasp that although I was intellectually prepared for Cambridge, nothing had prepared me socially. Many girls there knew other girls from their school or other girls' parents. I knew no one. Black and working-class, I was doubly an outsider. In my first year I was so lonely and so miserable that I regretted ever applying. My personal age of innocence about the British class system was over. I learned that far from being a comic anachronism, the British ruling class was alive and well and sending its children to Oxbridge. The simplest things astounded me. I remember the first time I sat at dinner and heard a girl casually discussing her family's cottage in the country. She might as well have talked about having a dacha on Mars. Nobody I knew had a country cottage. It was ridiculous. I remember meeting a history teacher and being offered a glass of wine. I came away tipsy with alcohol and excitement. This was the glamorous Oxbridge life I had read about. Drinking wine; and in the middle of the day! But I am not nostalgic about it in the accepted sense. I made only two lasting friendships, left it without a backward glance and have been back only three times.

But it was not a mistake to go. After the deep misery of my

first year I cheered up and started to enjoy it a little. It could have broken me, but for better or worse, it made me. Having been effortlessly near the top of my class all my life, I was in the company of girls who had all been effortlessly top and I realised that whatever else I was, I was not an academic. But the knowledge that I had got there, starting out with almost every conceivable disadvantage, in competition with girls with every advantage, gave me a life-long confidence. I learned a little history and a lot about social ritual. I learned how to survive in a white, establishment institution. And in a general sense I learned 'the rules'. Quite what 'the rules' are it is difficult to say. The unwritten codes and regulations that govern social interaction in the English ruling class will do as a working definition. What I found in later life was that people don't necessarily expect you to play by the rules. But it helps if they know that you know what they are. I graduated from Cambridge and went on to have some widely differing employers: the Home Office, Lambeth Council, TV AM, the National Council for Civil Liberties, the union ACTT and the late Greater London Council. What they all had in common was that every interview panel had a fellow Oxbridge graduate on it.

Cambridge didn't transform me; in some ways it was a disappointment. And the idyllic undergraduate life of my dreams firmly eluded me.

Furthermore, my political life has been devoted to reforming the power structure which Oxbridge revealed to me and of which it is a linchpin.

But the decision to go for unknown horizons; that was my transforming moment. And the refusal to accept other people's definitions of me, and the stubborn belief that I could be whatever I wanted to be, were to take me eventually all the way to the House of Commons.

## Other Virago Upstarts

### Bitter-Sweet Dreams

Girls' and Young Women's Own Stories

By the readers of *Just Seventeen*

'It's about time you let us have our say.' This reply from a Merseyside girl was echoed by teenagers across Britain who responded to Virago's invitation in *Just Seventeen* magazine to paint a picture of what their lives are like. The result is riveting and sobering. Consuming details of daily life – exams and jobs, clothes and friends – contrast with their own cautionary tales of young mothers, drugs and restless lives. Family and love dominate, and faced with the reality of unemployment, many write longingly of their desire for 'a brilliant career'. Clear-eyed, plain-speaking, wistful yet knowing, here are the bitter-sweet dreams of the eighties generation.

### Nell's Quilt

Susan Terris

When eighteen-years-old Nell reluctantly agrees to marry the widower her parents have chosen for her, she gives up her dreams of going to college and following in her suffragist grandmother's footsteps. That spring day, in 1899, she begins to piece and embroider a quilt. And she virtually stops eating. Soon the quilt consumes her days and as she makes it more and more beautiful, Nell, in contrast, grows frailer. This is 'enthralling dramatisation of the need for self-definition' *(Kirkus)*, powerful and exquisitely written, won the 1987 Commonwealth Silver Medal Juvenile Literature Award. **Susan Terris** lives in San Fransisco and is the author of many books for children and teenagers.

## The Comic Book of First Love

### Edited by PHILIP BOYS and CORINNE PEARLMAN

First love is exhilarating, embarrassing, engrossing — and unforgettable. In this wonderful collection, women and men cartoonists conjure up all the heady and agonising aspects of that first big heart-throb. Here are some of Britain's best illustrators and cartoonists, including Biff, Ann Braybon, Kate Charlesworth, Caroline Della Porta, Myra Hancock, Cliff Harper, Graham Higgins, David Hine, Julie Hollings, Rian Hughes, Natacha Ledwidge, Viv Quillin, Posy Simmonds, Suzy Varty. They look at jealousy and best friends; flirtation and unrequited love; infatuation with the famous, the fictional and the 'unsuitable'. For those who are about to take the plunge, for those who've already jumped and for those back on dry land, this book is for you.

### Annie on my Mind

#### Nancy Garden

When Liza Winthrop first meets Annie Kenyon in the Metropolitan Museum of Art, she knows something important is happening. Both seventeen years old, from opposite sides of New York, from two very different families — one working-class Italian, one middle-class and all-American — their chance meeting begins a wonderful, absorbing romance. Together they explore each other's New York: Brooklyn Heights, Uptown, the Cloisters, Coney Island — growing ever closer until suddenly and very painfully their relationship is put on trial by parents and school. This tender, funny and bitter-sweet love story was chosen by the American Library Association as one of the Best Books for Young Adults.

**Nancy Garden** lives in New York. After many years working in the theatre, she now writes full time.

Send a S.A.E. for our complete list.